Learning to Think and Choose:

Decision-making Episodes for the Middle Grades

OTHER GOOD YEAR® BOOKS IN THIS SERIES

Good Year Books

are available for most basic curriculum subjects plus many enrichment areas. For more Good Year Books, contact your local bookseller or educational dealer. For a complete catalog with information about other Good Year Books, please write:

Good Year Books
Department GYB
1900 East Lake Avenue
Glenview, Illinois 60025

Learning to Think and Choose:
Decision-making Episodes for the Middle Grades

J. Doyle Casteel
Professor of Education
University of Florida, Gainesville

Scott, Foresman and Company
Glenview, Illinois
Dallas, TX
Oakland, NJ
Palo Alto, CA
Tucker, GA
London, England

For

Little Bit *(Lonia Leah)*
Jim Boy *(James Paul)*
Bird *(Sharon Denise)*

My children, each of whom I love very much.

Contents

Learning to Think and Choose:
Decision-making Episodes for the Middle Grades

Introduction: Some Objectives, Definitions, Assumptions, and a Sporting Proposition

Helping students acquire and practice the use of valuing skills is and should be a basic goal of instruction in grades five, six, seven, and eight. The central purpose of *Learning to Think and Choose: Decision-making Episodes for the Middle Grades* is to present middle-grade teachers and teacher trainees with one approach that they may employ in order to address themselves to this goal. The approach presented presumes that those who teach such classes as English, science, and the social studies can and will use strategies that are consistent with their responsibility to teach significant and valid ideas, concepts, and themes derived from academic areas of study such as biology, sociology, or literature.

Specific Objectives

Learning to Think and Choose is a how-to-do-it book.[1] Six specific objectives have influenced the way in which this book is organized. These objectives are:

1. To describe and present examples of five different types of value clarification activities that middle-grade teachers may use in order to help students acquire and practice the use of valuing skills.

2. To present materials that middle-grade teachers may use in order to assess the practicality of

---

[1]The approach presented is derived from a theoretical model of verbal classroom discourse. This model is presented and described in: J. Doyle Casteel and Robert J. Stahl, *The Social Science Observation Record: Theoretical Model and Pilot Studies*, 1973. Copies may be secured by writing to Dr. J. B. Hodges, Director; the P. K. Yonge School; University of Florida; Gainesville, Florida 32611.

the different types of value clarification activities described and presented.

3. To provide decision-making activities related to three social processes that tend to be present in any group, including those groups that structure themselves in the classroom—namely, the processes of conflict, cooperation, and competition.

4. To provide decision-making exercises related to two social conditions the middle-grade student is likely to encounter with some frequency—namely, power and relative deprivation.

5. To delineate one approach that teachers may use in order to employ each type of value clarification exercise presented.

6. To identify and sequence the steps that one takes in order to develop original value clarification exercises of different types.

Valuing Skills

Valuing skills applicable in decision-making situations may be identified and defined.[2] Five of these valuing skills are:

1. Policy skill
2. Consequential skill
3. Outcome skill
4. Criterial skill
5. Emotive skill

These five skills are defined on the following pages in terms of learning conditions and anticipated student responses (Figures 1–5). For each of the five skills, the learning conditions one would create in order to elicit desired student behavior are listed to the left; the initial stu-

---

[2]Generic learning skills such as listening, observing, reading, recording, and communicating are, of course, important aspects of decision making. The intent here, however, is to define different acts of valuation with some precision and from the perspective of the classroom.

dent behavior sought within these learning conditions is listed to the right. If the behavior listed to the right occurs in response to the conditions to the left, then the skill identified is said to be displayed by the student.[3]

---

[3]These definitions were first published in a slightly different form: J. Doyle Casteel and Miriam Williford, *Planning Cross-Cultural Lessons*, 1975. A National Seminar Publication of the Latin American Studies Association.

Figure 1: **Policy Skill Defined in Terms of Learning Conditions and Critical Student Response Behavior**

Learning Conditions to be Established

1. Presentation of a social situation in which an individual or a group needs to make a decision.
2. Provision of a policy that *is* relevant to the social situation presented.
3. Two or three policies, *none* of which are relevant to the social situation presented.
4. Directions to the effect that students are to identify the one policy that *is* relevant to the social situation presented.

Student Response Behavior
Students will identify the one policy that is relevant to the given social situation.

Figure 2: **Consequential Skill Defined in Terms of Learning Conditions and Critical Student Response Behavior**

Learning Conditions to be Established

1. A social situation in which an individual or a group has been required to make a decision is presented.
2. The decision made by the individual or group in the social situation is identified and described.
3. One set of three or four results, i.e., consequences, *likely* to eventuate from the decision made in the given situation, is provided.
4. Two or three other sets of results, unlikely to eventuate from the decision made in the given situation, are provided.
5. Directions to the effect that students are to identify the *one* set of results likely to occur as a result of the decision made in the given social situation.

Student Response Behavior
Students will select the one set of consequences most likely to result from the decision made in the social situation presented.

Figure 3: *Outcome Skill Defined in Terms of Learning Conditions and Critical Student Response Behavior*

Learning Conditions to be Established

1. An end or outcome that an individual or group wishes to achieve is identified. (This end is easy to visualize, e.g., to own a bicycle, be chosen as a cheerleader, or to win a prize in a contest.)
2. A social situation providing a context within which the outcome desired is to be sought by an individual or group is presented.
3. One policy relevant to the social situation presented and likely to enable the person or group to attain the desired outcome is provided.
4. Two or three policies, all relevant to the social situation presented but unlikely to yield the desired outcome, are provided.
5. Directions to the effect that students are to identify the *one* policy likely to yield the desired outcome.

Student Response Behavior

Students will select the one policy that is likely to yield the desired outcome within the context of the given social situation.

Figure 4: *Criterial Skill Defined in Terms of Learning Conditions and Critical Student Response Behavior*

Learning Conditions to be Established

1. A criterion that is to be applied in order to make a decision is presented and explained. (The criterion is relatively abstract, e.g., fairness, justice, loyalty, reciprocity.)
2. A social situation in which a decision is to be made is presented.
3. One policy, germane to the given social situation and *consistent* with the standard of judgment that is to be applied, is provided.
4. Two or three policies, relevant to the given social situation but *inconsistent* with the standard of judgment that is to be applied, are presented.
5. Directions to the effect that students are to identify the *one* policy that is consistent with the given criterion.

Student Response Behavior

Students will select the *one* policy that is consistent with the criterion that has been given as the standard of judgment to be applied in the social situation presented.

Figure 5: Emotive Skill Defined in Terms of Learning Conditions and Critical Student Response Behavior

**Learning Conditions
to be Established**

1. An emotional state is identified and explained, e.g., love, desire, jealousy, envy, or rage.
2. A social situation in which an individual or group needs to make a decision is presented.
3. One option, *likely* to be adopted by an individual who is experiencing the given emotional state, is provided.
4. Two or three options, relevant to the given social situation but *unlikely* to be adopted by a person who is experiencing the given emotional state, are provided.
5. Directions to the effect that students are to select the one policy likely to be adopted by an individual experiencing the given emotional state.

**Student
Response Behavior**
Students will select the *one* policy likely to be opted for by an individual experiencing the given emotional state within the context of the social situation given.

Value Sheets

One of the means by which you may help students acquire and refine valuing skills is to select or write value sheets relevant to the content being taught. Value sheets are learning activities that are so structured as to create learning conditions in which students, working in small groups, are likely to exhibit two or more of the five valuing skills identified above and defined in Figures 1–5.

Value sheets written in five formats will be presented in subsequent chapters. Each chapter will consist of five sections, in the following order:

Section 1.   *Functions of the format of the value sheet presented in each chapter.*

Section 2.   *A description of the components that are used to build the type of value sheets presented in each chapter.*

Section 3.   *Classroom examples of the format developed in each chapter.*

Section 4.   *From the teacher's perspective*, one approach that the middle-grade teacher might employ in order to use the examples presented in each chapter.

Section 5.   *On your own*, a presentation of step-by-step directions that teachers might follow in order to develop their own examples of the format presented in each chapter.

Some Assumptions

Several assumptions are made with regard to value clarification. Some of these are presented here, not to convince so much as to forewarn.

Assumption 1.   *Decision making is tied to understanding.* If an issue or a situation is comprehended poorly, the decisions made are unlikely to be wise no matter how adequately valuing skills are applied. Each of the value sheets presented in subsequent chapters is focused on a social situation presented in the guise of a short story. Students must comprehend this situation if the value sheet is to work as intended.

Assumption 2.   *Instructional materials are not intended to teach. Rather, they are instruments to be used by teachers.* It is the teacher who selects or writes a value sheet for student use; who provides directions that help students perceive purpose in what they are doing; who monitors student behavior and maintains a learning climate; who organizes students into learning groups; and who provides feedback on student performance. In common with other instructional resources, value sheets are a tool for teaching, not a substitute. Although each chapter contains a section in which one approach is delineated, this section should be read in the light of this assumption and not as a prescription.

Assumption 3. *To function most effectively, instructional materials must be made relevant to two worlds of experience.* The child lives in a world of experience in which certain events and situations appear important to him. Instructional materials designed for middle-grade pupils should focus on this world and draw on the student's interest. At the same time, there are societal events and situations that may be referred to as the adult's world of experience. The value sheets used to exemplify different types of value clarification activities in the chapters that follow are intended to present significant adult concerns in terms of events and situations that belong to the child's world of experience.

Assumption 4. *Decision making and the study of organized bodies of knowledge, such as science or history or literature, may be and ought to be coordinated.* What one learns in science may be made applicable to such topics as the quality of our environment or the energy crisis by placing students in decision-making situations in which they have an opportunity to display and use their knowledge and understanding. And using such knowledge in decision-making episodes that are made relevant to the students' world of experience provides these students with an opportunity to perceive that such knowledge and understanding have personal and social utility. The value sheets that appear in subsequent chapters are related to personal and social dimensions of five concepts—cooperation, conflict, competition, power, and relative deprivation. Teachers who write their own value sheets may relate them to concepts they are teaching, topics they are exploring, themes they are examining, issues they are analyzing, or ideas and principles they are asking students to validate.

Assumption 5. *The classroom teacher should not hesitate to create and maintain structures that are likely to eventuate in desired student learnings.* It is sometimes argued that if teachers talked less and students talked more, students would learn more and have more interest in school. It is also asserted that if a teacher can ask good questions, then he is likely to experience teaching success. Neither of these contentions is valid. While the teacher may structure so frequently as to inhibit or bar student behavior, he is responsible for creating learning conditions, including constraints, within which it is believed students will learn. While teachers frequently employ questions to solicit desired student behaviors, they do so within a structured learning situation. The assumption that the teacher should structure learning conditions is most obvious in the sections entitled "From the Teacher's Perspective" in subsequent chapters. There, importance is placed on providing learning set, learning closure, and on how to give careful directions.

Assumption 6.   *Values and valuing skills are learned, maintained, and rejected or modified in groups.* For this reason, the value sheets provided in Chapters 2–5 contain at least two decision sheets. The first decision sheet is to be used by students individually in order to react personally to a social situation. The second decision sheet is to be used by students in organized groups of four to five members. Hence, if initial and individual reactions differ, these differences must be resolved in order to complete the group decision sheet. Stated another way, the group decision sheet triggers value clarification behavior, as discussed above, because initial reactions to situations become an aspect of the valuing exercise and are subjected to the scrutiny, criticism, and use of the group.

A Sporting Proposition

Prior to studying subsequent chapters, you are invited to test the utility of the approach presented. In order to determine whether or not the use of value sheets with small groups of students will result in student use of valuing skills, take the following steps:

- O Choose one of the value sheets presented in Chapter 2.
- O Make five or six copies of the value sheet.
- O Secure a cassette recorder and a tape.
- O Select a group of four or five students.
     Ask them to study the social situation at the focus of the value sheet you selected. (Do not distribute the decision sheets yet.)
- O Ascertain that students have understood the social situation.
- O Ask students to complete the individual decision sheet.

○ Turn the recorder on to record.
○ Explain that students are to share individual reactions and then to seek consensus. (You may need to explain what it means to seek consensus.)
○ Ask students to work together in order to complete the group decision sheet.
○ Dismiss the students and rewind the tape.
○ Listen to the tape in order to answer these questions:

Did students use *policy* skill?
Did students use *consequential* skill?
Did students use *criterial* skill?
Did students use *outcome* skill?
Did students use *emotive* skill?

○ Determine the degree to which the value sheet worked for you.
○ Now that you've observed for yourself how value sheets elicit the use of valuing skills from decision-making groups, you're ready to study the chapters that follow.

1 The Standard Format of the Value Sheet

Functions

The standard format of the value sheet emphasizes that there is a personal form of knowing and understanding. Although knowledge and understanding are acquired in numerous ways, the process of information acquisition and processing may be clarified by referring to three levels of reading for knowledge and understanding.

A poem, novel, newspaper article, or book may be read in order to comprehend what the author has to say within the context in which he chose to communicate with his reader. The objective in this case is to comprehend—referred to as a *comprehension* level of learning.

Or, a poem, novel, newspaper article, or book may be read in order to enhance the understanding of an issue, idea, topic, theme, or concept. In this case, one must understand what the author expressed in his context. But those elements of the author's message that are relevant to the issue must also be identified and attended to—the idea, topic, theme, or concept that should be understood better as a result of reading. The objective in this case is, at the least, to analyze; and such analysis may lead to synthesis and evaluation. Together, they are referred to as an *analytical* level of information acquisition and processing.

A poem, novel, newspaper article, or book may also be read in order to clarify a personal position with regard to social issues and situations. In this case, the author's message must first be understood in context. Such understanding tends to be enhanced if the author's message is analyzed. But the primary objective is to clarify a person's beliefs with regard to social issues and situations. The objective here is to gain insight into beliefs and commitments—or, a *personal* level of learning.

The standard format of the value sheet is intended to elicit these three types of behavior from students: comprehension, analysis, and personalization of information and ideas.

Description

The standard format of the value sheet contains four components: (1) a social situation; (2) comprehension directions and questions; (3) relational directions and questions; and (4) value/feeling directions and questions.

The social situation may be created in a variety of ways. Select a section from a play, novel, or short story that is relevant to the topic, concept, or idea that you are teaching; select a cartoon, picture, graph, or a table of statistical data that is relevant to the topic, concept, theme, or idea that you are teaching; or, select a current-events article from a magazine or newspaper that is relevant to the current focus of class study. Also select recordings of songs or speeches and use these to establish a social situation. Develop an instructional resource and use this to establish a stimulus situation. Or, you may choose to write social situations that reflect the behavior and concerns of the class.

The social situation, regardless of its source or form, is selected and used on three grounds. First, it must be relevant to the current focus of study in the class in which it is to be used. Consequently, a source might be useful in a history class but not relevant to the focus of study in a biology class. Second, the resource must be one from which students can acquire information and interpret in relation to the content they are studying at the time the value sheet is used. Third, the resource must be one that deals with an event, situation, or set of behaviors toward which students can form preferences and express personal reactions.

The second component of the standard format of the value sheet consists of five or six comprehension discussion starters. Discussion starters are directions or questions that students may respond to in order to study the social situation and acquire information. Some conventions, according to which comprehension discussion starters may be written, are:

> *Who* was present?
> *Who* was involved?
> *Who* acted first?
> *When* did this event occur?
> *When* did he leave?
> *When* did he become upset?
> Describe the hallway where the fight occurred.
> List the places that she went.
> *Where* did the action occur?
> *Where* was he going?
> *What* was her goal?
> *What* did John do?
> Describe the object that Lisa found.
> *How long* did it take the man to act?
> For *how long* did the woman believe this?
> *How much* money was involved?
> *How much* time was spent?
> *How many* people were present?
> *How many* days did it take?

These conventions may be summarized: Ask questions beginning with the words *who, when, where, what, how long, how much,* and *how many* that can be answered by referring to the stimulus situation with which students are provided.

Other conventions, according to which comprehension discussion starters may be phrased, are:

Quote a line or two from the stimulus situation;
Ask students to express the meaning of the quota-
tion in their own words.

Focus attention on a paragraph or an element of a
picture or song;
Ask students questions—who, when, where, what,
how long, how much, and how many.

Quote a selection from the stimulus situation;
Cite a word or phrase used in the source;
Ask students to define the word or term using the
context provided in the situation.

Define a word or phrase that is used in the stimulus
situation;
Ask students to volunteer illustrations consistent
with the definition you gave.

The third component of a standard format of the value sheet consists of two to four relational discussion starters. These are questions or directions that enable students to frame relationships between the information and knowledge presented in the stimulus situation and the topic, theme, concept, or idea they are currently studying. In effect, students use relational discussion starters to search for elements that may be made relevant to what they are currently studying in the class where the standard format of the value sheet is used.

Some conventions, according to which relational discussion starters may be written, are:

Define the concept at the focus of study;
Ask students to find an example of the concept in the
social situation.

Define the concept at the focus of study;
Cite an instance of behavior in the social situation;
Ask students to explain why the behavior is an ex-
ample of the concept.

Cite the theme you are teaching, e.g., fear;
Ask students how the theme is reflected in the social situation.

Cite the theme you are teaching;
Review with students how this theme was presented in a resource previously studied;
Review with students how the theme is presented in the current social situation;
Ask students how the two presentations differ; or,
Ask students how the two presentations are similar.

Cite the theme you are teaching;
Cite an element of the social situation;
Ask students how the element cited presents an aspect of the theme that is being studied.

Suggest a number of themes you have taught;
Cite an instance of behavior in the social situation;
Ask students to identify the theme that is depicted by the instance cited.

Cite the idea you are teaching;
Cite data presented in the social situation;
Ask students how the data supports the idea.

Cite the idea you are teaching;
Cite data presented in the social situation;
Ask students how the data might be used to question the validity of the idea being taught.

Ask students to state the idea at the focus of study;
Ask students to then identify elements of the social situation that support the idea; or,
Ask students to then identify elements of the social situation that might be used to question the validity of the idea.

Ask students to identify the idea at the focus of study;

Point out an idea that is presented in the social situation;

Ask students how the two ideas differ or are similar.

Ask students to define the concept at the focus of study;

Point out an instance of behavior in the social situation;

Ask students to explain why the instance of behavior is an example of the concept.

Define or ask students to define the concept at the focus of study;

Point out an instance of behavior in the social situation;

Ask students if the instance is an example of the concept at the focus of study.

(Affirmatively, after students have so responded, wait, saying nothing, in order that they may volunteer statements as to how they reasoned; if they fail to do so, probe to secure an explanation.)

Define or ask students to define the concept at the focus of study;

Cite an instance of behavior presented in the social situation;

Ask students to explain why the behavior cited is not an example of the concept.

Cite the topic you are teaching;

Ask students to identify aspects of the social situation that are relevant to the topic.

Identify the topic that is the current focus of study;

Point out an aspect of the social situation;

Ask students why the aspect is relevant.

Ask students to identify the topic that is at the focus of study;

Point out one aspect of the social situation;

Ask students how the aspect pointed out is relevant to the current topic of study.

Identify the topic that is the focus of study;
Designate one aspect of the social situation;
Ask students to explain why the aspect cited is not relevant to the topic of study.

Similar conventions may be used if a standard format of the value sheet in reference to an issue that is being analyzed or a principle that is being validated by students is assigned. Observe that the function of these conventions is to help students frame relationships between the social situation used to construct the standard format of the value sheet and the concept, topic, theme, or idea that is currently being studied by students who are asked to respond to the value sheet.

The fourth and final component of a standard format of the value sheet consists of value/feeling discussion starters. Value/feeling discussion starters are questions and directions that encourage students to react to the stimulus situation, as understood in response to comprehension and relational discussion starters, by expressing personal preferences; considering what might be or what should be done in the situation; exploring the consequences of events or possible options that might be exercised; identifying criteria that might be used to justify different courses of action; or sharing personal feelings.

Some of the conventions that you may employ in order to write value/feeling discussion starters are presented here. Some of these conventions are likely to result in one- or two-word responses. In such cases, after this initial response wait to see if students explain or clarify their answers. If students fail to do so, given this opportunity to explain or clarify, request that they provide explanations or clarifications. Conventions, according to which value/feeling discussion starters may be written, are:

Cite or describe a social condition;
Ask students if the condition is good.

Cite or describe a social condition;
Ask students if the condition is bad.

Cite or describe two or more social conditions;
Ask students which condition is best.

Cite or describe two or more social conditions;
Ask students which condition is worst.

Cite or describe a social problem;
Place a student within this problem situation;
Ask the student what might be done in order to re-solve the problem.

Cite or describe a social condition;
Ask a student to imagine he is involved;
Ask the student what he would do.

Cite or describe a social situation;
Cite or describe a procedure that might be used in this situation;
Ask students to identify probable consequences.

Describe an emotional state;
Describe a social situation;
Ask students how the emotional state might influence behavior in the situation given.

Cite or describe an emotional state;
Cite or describe a social situation;
Place a student within this condition;
Ask the student if the emotional state is good; or,
Ask the student if the emotional state is bad.

Describe a social problem;
Cite a policy that has been selected;
Place the student within this condition;
Ask the student to demonstrate that the policy adopted is reasonable; or,
Ask a student to demonstrate that the policy is unreasonable.

Value/feeling discussion starters that are written according to these conventions are intended to allow students to personalize their understanding of standard types of resources that are typically used in the classroom; hence the name, *standard format of the value sheet.*

Classroom Examples

Ten examples of the standard format of the value sheet are provided here. Study at least four of these, paying particular attention to the student behaviors most likely to be elicited by the discussion starters. This approach should enable you to understand the sections dealing with the use and construction of standard format examples of the value sheet.

tom's duty

Conceptual focus: Conflict

SOCIAL SITUATION

Tom Jones is a very good football player. As a linebacker, he has helped his team win six games. They have lost only once and one game remains to be played.

This Saturday, Tom's team will play another good team. The other team has also won six games and also has one tie on its record.

If Tom's team wins, they will be champions of the recreation league. If they lose, then the other team will be champions.

Tom is looking forward to the game. He is a loyal member of his team.

Tom is also a school leader. Tom wants his school to be one of the very best schools. Last week the principal asked him to serve on a committee.

The principal said, "Tom, it is time we took a look at the school handbook. As you know, we use the handbook to introduce new students to our school. We need students like you to revise it."

Tom was pleased that he was asked to serve on the committee. He quickly agreed to do what the principal asked.

He said, "I would like to be on the committee. When will we meet?"

The principal answered, "The first and most important meeting is next Monday, right after school. It is very important that all committee members be present for that meeting."

"I'll be there," Tom said.

On Friday, it rained all day. Early Saturday morning, Tom's football coach called him.

The coach said, "Tom, we aren't playing today. The field is flooded. We'll play for the championship on Monday afternoon, right after school is dismissed. See you then."

After hanging up the phone, Tom thought, "Gosh. I forgot. I promised the principal I would attend a committee meeting on Monday night."

Tom then called his school principal. The principal said, "It's too bad that both the game and the meeting are scheduled for the same time. It's too late to change the meeting. I'm afraid you'll have to choose which event is more important to you."

Tom answered, "I feel bad about this. But I'm going to play in the football game."

Even as he spoke, Tom was very unhappy. One part of him wanted to play in the game, and another part wanted to attend the committee meeting.

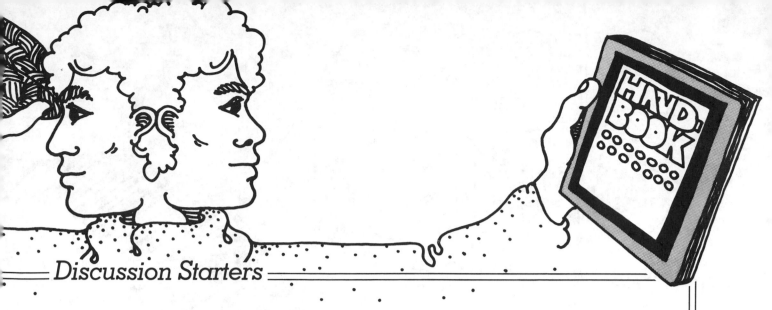

Discussion Starters

COMPREHENSION

1. What game does Tom play?
2. How good is Tom's team?
3. How many games has the other team won?
4. When was Tom's team supposed to play?
5. Why was the game delayed?
6. Tom agrees to become a member of the school committee. What is the purpose of the committee?

RELATIONAL

7. Tom decides to play in the game. How does this conflict with what the principal expected?
8. Suppose Tom had decided to attend the meeting. How might this have caused conflict with the other members of his team?
9. Tom wants to be loyal to his team. Tom wants to be loyal to his school. How are his two desires in conflict?

VALUE/FEELING

10. Tom decided to play in the football game. Was this a good decision?
11. If you had been Tom, what would you have done?
12. If you had made the decision Tom made, how would you have felt?

SUE'S AMBITION

Conceptual focus: Conflict

SOCIAL SITUATION

Sue is an ambitious girl, and wants to be an excellent student. She wants to learn to play the piano quite well. She is a member of a girls' club and wants to be a leader.

Sue is also talented, and can be an excellent student. She can, with practice, play the piano very well; and she serves as leader in her social club.

All her life, Sue has made one mistake. She has often tried to do too many things at once which prevents her from doing any of them as well as she might.

Take this afternoon—Sue's interests caught up with her. In order to prepare for school tomorrow, she must finish a book report for English, study for a science test, and complete her geography assignment.

Sue was also supposed to go for a piano lesson and attend a meeting of her social club.

Not knowing what to do, Sue told her mother she was ill and went to bed.

Discussion Starters

COMPREHENSION

1. Sue wants to do three things. Name them.
2. What school assignments is Sue supposed to finish this evening?
3. Besides preparing for school, what else does Sue need to do today?
4. What bad mistake does Sue often make?
5. What does Sue decide to do?

RELATIONAL

6. This afternoon, Sue's desire to be a good student is in conflict with her desire to play the piano well. Why?
7. Suppose Sue also wants to be honest with her mother. To what extent is Sue's statement that she is ill in conflict with her desire to be honest?
8. Sue wants to be good at all that she does. Sue tries to do more than she should attempt. How is her behavior in conflict with her desire?

VALUE/FEELING

9. Sue went to bed rather than try to do all the things she could not hope to get done. If you were Sue, what would you have done?
10. Suppose you were Sue. If you were, what would you do to avoid this problem in the future?
11. If you were Sue, how would you explain your failure to have your work done when you attend school tomorrow?

Bouncers, Fly Balls Butterfingers, and Victories

Conceptual focus: Cooperation

SOCIAL SITUATION

At Elm Creek Middle School, it was a hot day. It was already hot in Mrs. Blur's class when the school day began. By 11:00 A.M. students were so hot they could hardly listen to Mrs. Blur. Trying with all their might, it was hard to pay attention. By early afternoon, it was almost impossible to breathe in the room.

Mrs. Blur said, "We've got to get out of here. I'll tell you what. Let's go outside and play softball."

Some of Mrs. Blur's students liked this idea. They said, "You're a great thinker, Mrs. Blur."

Some of the other students, however, did not like the idea. And they shared their feelings with other students.

"It's too hot to play softball."

"It's too dirty out there."

"The gnats and flies will eat us alive."

"You've got to be joking."

Mrs. Blur responded, "Whatever we do, we'll have to do together."

Bob, one of the students, said, "Why don't we all go outside? It's cooler there. Those who want to play softball can play. Those who don't want to play can talk with each other, or they can watch the game."

Everyone agreed with Bob's idea. Soon, twenty of Mrs. Blur's students had chosen teams and were playing.

For the first two innings, everyone was happy. Then in the top of the third inning, things began to go wrong.

The first batter hit a high bouncer to the second baseman. Tony, the second baseman, knew it was a sure out. But he took his eye off the ball. The ball hit the fingertips of his glove and bounced away. The runner was safe.

Cindy yelled at Tony, "Butterfingers!"

Greg said, "Who told you you knew how to play?"

Linda got into the act: "Which team are you playing for? Ours or theirs?"

The next batter hit a soft fly ball in the direction of Susan. Susan lost the ball in the sun. This put runners on second and third.

Tony was the first to speak. "Girls shouldn't be allowed to play this game. They've all got butterfingers. They can't catch. They can't hit. They can't run. The only thing they know how to do is lose."

Cindy answered Tony. "Look at the person who's doing the talking!"

Soon, most the boys and girls on the team were shouting at each other.

Mrs. Blur blew her whistle. Gradually, the boys and girls became quiet.

Mrs. Blur asked the members of the teams in the field to form a small circle around her. When the twenty boys and girls were ready, Mrs. Blur made a little speech.

"In order to have fun when you play a team sport, you must cooperate; to win, you must cooperate; to play any team game well, all members of a team must support all other team members.

"If we cannot play the game correctly, we'll have to go back inside. I don't want to go back. And I don't believe you want to go back to that hot room.

"When a member of your team makes a mistake, that person needs your support. If a team member does well, he can support himself. Do you understand?"

"Yes, we do," was the response of the twenty students.

Members of the two teams continued to play for about another hour. Tony had a lot of chances at ground balls; he didn't make another error, and Susan also played well.

When the game was over, the other team was ahead by a score of 13 to 11.

"They won," Susan said.

"But it was close," Tony added.

Hearing Tony and Susan talk as the students were returning to the classroom, Mrs. Blur said, "Your team won something, too."

The Standard Format of the Value Sheet   25

Discussion Starters

COMPREHENSION

1. Why does Mrs. Blur want to leave her classroom?
2. When Mrs. Blur suggests playing a game, some of her students disagree. Why don't they want to play?
3. How is the argument over going outside settled?
4. After the game started, there was an argument. What caused this argument?

RELATIONAL

5. When people work together to secure a common goal, they cooperate. Mrs. Blur says that all team sports require cooperation. Do you agree? (Be prepared to explain your answer.)
6. Mrs. Blur also insists that her class cooperate before students are allowed to go outside. Name some ways in which class members can cooperate.

VALUE/FEELING

7. Mrs. Blur says it is good to help people when they make a mistake. Would you help a teammate who made a mistake? Would you want to support a person who cost your team a big game?
8. Suppose you wanted to help a person who made a mistake that cost your team a big game. How might you help the person who made the mistake?
9. Let's say you are one of the girls who chose not to play. When Susan fails to catch the ball, Tony says girls should not be allowed to play. When Tony says this, how do you feel?
10. Mrs. Blur said, "We'll play as a team or we'll all go inside." Was this a good way to handle the problem? (Be prepared to justify your response.)

When Two Oxen Are Stuck in the Mud

Conceptual focus: Cooperation

SOCIAL SITUATION

Once upon a time, there was a planet called Luxor. On the planet of Luxor, there was a land called Luxland.

The people of Luxland were a simple but happy group of people. Most of them lived in villages located in the valleys of the vast mountains. Most Luxlanders earned their living by farming. In each village, there were craftspeople who made shoes, ox harnesses, and tools that the farmers used. Most frequently, Luxlanders traded what they grew for the things these village craftspeople made for them.

The Luxlanders who lived in villages seldom used money. Sometimes they had a few pieces of gold or silver. Since they had no money, Luxlanders did not ask a craftsperson how much a cart for hauling crops would cost in money. Instead, Luxlanders asked, ''How many oxen will you accept in exchange for this cart?''

Each year, the villagers of Luxland sent some of the grain they had grown to the one city in Luxland, Lux City. All the farmers of a village got together and chose one man to go to the city. He kept a careful record of how much grain each man gave him to take to the market in Lux City. He also kept a careful record of what each person wanted from the city. To be chosen to make this trip was a great honor and a great responsibility.

One year when the crops were good, Ulford was selected by his village to go to the city. He loaded his cart and set off for the city. Normally, it would take him three days to reach the city. Ulford knew it would be a longer trip that year.

The rains had been heavy. In the mountains that he must cross many of the roads would be damaged. This would slow him down.

When the roads wound through valleys, the valley roads would be soft and muddy. Such heavy going would slow his dependable oxen.

The crops had been especially good that year. So, Ulford was carrying more grain than was usually taken to the city.

By the third day, Ulford was a little over half way to Lux City. He came to a place where three village roads met. At this junction, Ulford reached the main highway to Lux City.

About the time that Ulford reached this junction, carts from two other villages also arrived. Like Ulford's cart, these too were heavily loaded.

"Crops have been good in all villages this year," Ulford thought. "Grain will be plentiful in Lux City. Those who want grain will bargain hard. Perhaps I can beat the other carts to Lux City."

About five miles later, the main road to Lux City ran next to a stream. Although the road was open, Ulford could tell the road had recently been under water.

Ulford started across the flat area that had been flooded. Soon his cart was mired in mud, almost up to the axle. Ulford climbed down from his cart and tried to help his oxen. Even with his help the oxen could not move the cart.

Ulford did not know what to do. Looking over his shoulder he saw that the other carts had stopped when they saw that he was stuck.

Ulford waded through the mud back to the other carts. He said, "We'll never get through to Lux City."

The driver of one of the other carts said, "If we work together we can all get across this bad spot. First we'll use all six oxen to move your cart. Then we'll use all six to move the second cart. And finally, we'll use all six oxen to move my cart."

"That's great," Ulford said.

Using the six oxen, the three men moved their carts past the part of the road that had been flooded. Two days later, all three carts arrived in Lux City, one after the other. It was obvious to everyone that the three men driving the three teams of oxen were good friends who enjoyed one another's company.

Discussion Starters

COMPREHENSION

1. Describe the land of Luxland.
2. How do the people of Luxland earn a living?
3. When a Luxlander wants to buy something, what does he use instead of money?
4. Who is Ulford?
5. How is Ulford honored by the people of his village?
6. How does Ulford make friends with two men from villages other than his own?

RELATIONAL

7. When people work together to get something they all want, they cooperate. The village craftspeople and farmers cooperate to earn a living. How?
8. When people share resources, such as oxen, to succeed in doing something they all want to do, they cooperate. How do the three men cooperate in order to reach Lux City?
9. When people cooperate with one another, they are likely to trust and like one another. What parts of this story support this idea?

VALUE / FEELING

10. When Ulford first saw the two other villagers, he wanted to get to the city before they did. He hoped this would make his load of grain more valuable. Was this a good attitude?
11. Each year one man is chosen to go to Lux City. If you were helping to make the choice for your village, what type of person would you select?
12. Study your response to Question 11. Explain your answer.

A LOSER'S COMPLAINT

Conceptual focus: Competition

SOCIAL SITUATION

A school carnival was recently held at Robertsville Middle School. The purpose of the carnival was to raise money for the school. The teachers at Robertsville want to start a new reading program. To begin this new reading program, the teachers need new books, new filmstrips, and some new equipment.

At first, many of the teachers and most of the students were not very interested. Mr. Cobb, the principal, thought, "I must do something to cause interest in the carnival. Otherwise, we will not make enough money to start the new reading program."

After thinking about what he might do for a day, Mr. Cobb made an announcement:

"The sixth-grade class that makes the most money may have a popcorn party. The school will furnish the popcorn and pop.

"The seventh-grade class that makes the most money will be given free tickets to a college football game. The school will pay for the bus that will transport students to and from the game. The University has agreed to give us end-zone tickets.

"The eighth-grade class that makes the most money will be given free tickets to see a movie at one of the local theatres. Mr. Gomez, who owns the theatres, has given Robertsville tickets so that this prize may be offered."

Soon, all the classes at Robertsville began to work hard. Each class wanted to earn a prize.

When the carnival was held, Robertsville made a good profit. Students in classes that won prizes were very happy and those in classes that almost won but lost were very unhappy.

One member of a losing eighth-grade class stopped Mr. Cobb in the hallway. He said, "Mr. Cobb, your contest was unfair. My class worked hard. We earned a lot of money because we wanted to win a prize. We should get free movie tickets, even though we did not win."

Mr. Cobb was surprised. He replied, "Before the contest began, I announced the rules. The class that won, won according to those rules. When people compete for prizes, one group must win. Another group must lose. The contest was a fair one. I'm sorry you lost. But you must learn to be a good loser if you are going to get along in our society."

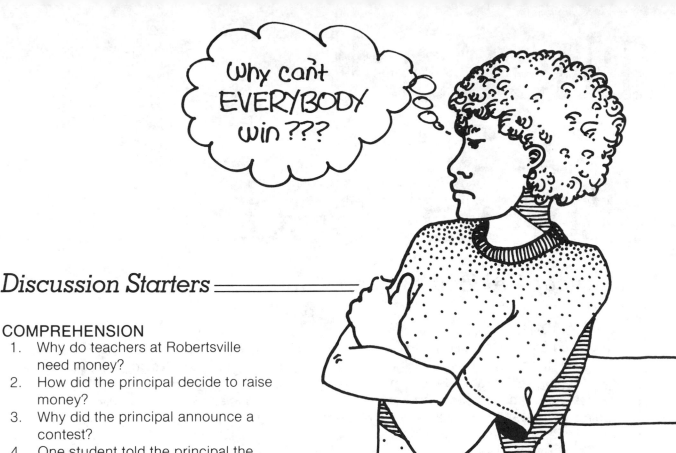

Discussion Starters

COMPREHENSION
1. Why do teachers at Robertsville need money?
2. How did the principal decide to raise money?
3. Why did the principal announce a contest?
4. One student told the principal the contest was unfair. Why did the student believe the contest was unfair?
5. The principal said the contest was fair. Why did he believe the contest was fair?

RELATIONAL
6. When different persons or groups try to obtain a goal and only one person or group can win, competition exists if everyone obeys the rules. Study this definition carefully. Did students at Robertsville compete with one another? (Be prepared to defend your answer.)
7. In this story students compete for prizes. What other good things do students compete for in school?
8. Students frequently compete for good grades. What are some of the rules they must obey if they are to win?

VALUE/FEELING
9. Robertsville holds a carnival to raise money to start a new school program. Suppose you wanted to argue that this is a *poor* way to get money for a school. What might you say?
10. Is it good to raise money for school purposes by holding carnivals? (Is your answer here consistent with your answer to Question 9?)
11. Students at Robertsville worked to earn prizes, not to start a new program. Is there anything wrong in this? (Be prepared to explain your response.)

The Cost of a Five-Speed

Conceptual focus: Competition

SOCIAL SITUATION

Doug and Steve live next door to each other. They are good friends.

Doug and Steve attend the same school. Each morning they ride to school together on their bikes. Each Saturday they ride their bikes to a movie.

This morning, Doug came for Steve early. He shouted, "Come on, Steve. There's a yard sale just two blocks away. They're supposed to be selling a five-speed bicycle. The ad said the bicycle is still in excellent shape."

When Doug and Steve arrived at the yard sale, the bicycle was still there—and it was in excellent shape.

"It looks as though it has never been ridden," Steve told Doug.

Doug agreed. "I want to buy it if I can. I hope I've got enough money."

Steve asked the owner, "How much is the bicycle?"

"As much as I can sell it for," the owner laughed.

"I've only got forty-three dollars," Doug said. "I'll give you forty-three dollars for the bike."

The owner thought about the offer. "That's not bad. I might take forty-three dollars. Let me think about it for a bit."

Steve jumped in. "Give me a chance, will you?" He added, "I've got fifty dollars. Will you take fifty dollars for the bike?"

"You bet," the owner replied. "Show me the money and you've got yourself a fine bicycle."

Steve bought the bicycle. He rode it all over his neighborhood showing it to the boys and girls he and Doug often play with.

As for Doug, he spent most of the day in his house. Just before he went in, he had a few words for his friend, Steve.

"I'm going to look for a new buddy. You're a fine friend. You took that bicycle away from me. I hope it breaks before the day is over. And don't you think I'm going to forget this. I'm going to remember what you did."

Discussion Starters

COMPREHENSION

1. Owning a good bicycle is important to both Doug and Steve. How do you know that this is true in the story?
2. How much does the owner want for the new bicycle?
3. How much does Doug offer for the bicycle?
4. Steve offers more for the bicycle. How much more does he offer?
5. What does Doug say in order to get even with Steve?
6. What does Steve do with the new bicycle?

RELATIONAL

7. When an owner offers to sell something that more than one person wants, he hopes the persons who want what he has for sale will *compete* with one another. To what extent does this happen in this story?
8. When two or more persons *compete* for the same thing they are supposed to obey rules. If any person who is competing breaks the rules, then conflict is likely. Does Steve break any rules that led to conflict with Doug? Explain your answer.
9. Refer to Question 8. Does Doug break any rules that led to conflict with Steve? Explain your answer.

VALUE/FEELING

10. Should Steve have offered more for the bicycle than Doug could offer?
11. Steve bought the bicycle. How is this likely to hurt Steve and Doug one week later?
12. The owner wanted to sell his bicycle for the highest price. Was his behavior wrong? Explain how you arrived at your answer.

PASS, PUNT,

Conceptual focus: Power

SOCIAL SITUATION

Paul, Billy, Jim, and Thad all live on the same street. They are all in the sixth grade and want to be football players and make the varsity team when they are in high school.

Last Christmas, each of the boys received a football. Since then, the boys have played football almost every day. They have used a vacant field at the end of the street.

The vacant field is a perfect place for the boys to play football. They can practice place-kicking. They can divide themselves into two teams and play a game of football. There are no windows to break, no flowers to trample, and no lawns to ruin. And, smaller children are not around to bother them, either.

Things were ideal until last month. Last month, the boys went to the field just as they always had. When they got there, they found that the whole field had been mowed. In addition, there were big signs all over the place:

Paul said, "Oh, no. Now we can't play in the field. We won't be able to play football any more."

Billy said, "Yes, we will. We'll play in Jim's yard."

Jim said, "We can't do that. My father says we ruin the lawn. My mother says we ruin her flower beds."

Thad said, "You're making a big deal out of this. They don't mean us. They mean hunters and those other boys who are always riding their motorcycles across the field."

Jim was suddenly happy. "That's right, Thad. Good thinking. Let's stop talking and play a game."

The boys began to play. About thirty minutes later, Paul looked up and spotted a police car.

Paul turned to Jim and said, "We're in trouble now."

Jim's answer was, "Let's get out of here."

The boys ran home. They never went to play in the field again.

The lady who owned the field had exercised her right, or power, to have the field mowed. She had used her power to put up signs telling other persons to stay out of the field. She had used her power to call the police. She could do this because she is a citizen and can demand police protection. As a property owner, she has controlled the behavior of Paul, Billy, Jim, and Thad.

AND TROUBLE

COMPREHENSION

1. What is the favorite game of the boys in this story?
2. Given the favorite game of the boys, why is the vacant field at the end of their street a perfect place to play?
3. Given that the boys think like boys usually think about having younger children around them, what makes the field a perfect place to play?

RELATIONAL

4. Persons sometimes do things to control the way we behave. When they do these things we say that they are using *power*. Given this definition of power, how does the woman who owns the field try to control the boys?
5. Billy wants to play football in Jim's yard. How does he try to use power over Jim?
6. In this story, how does Jim's father use *power*? Jim's mother?
7. If a person can do bad things to you, he may control your behavior. This is true even if he does nothing to hurt you. Given this definition of power, how does the policeman use power to control the four boys?

VALUE/FEELING

8. When the boys saw the signs in the field, what should they have done?
9. Suppose you were one of the four boys. If you were, what would you have done when you saw the signs?
10. Suppose you were one of the four boys. Assume the other boys got away but you did not. If this happened, what would you say to the policeman? To your "friends"?
11. Assume the lady who owned the field saw you playing football and called the police. Did she do the right thing? Explain your response.

Surprise, Surprise

Conceptual focus: Power

SOCIAL SITUATION

Ms. Phillips teaches fifth grade. For the last three days, teaching has not been fun for her. Before school began on Friday, Ms. Phillips decided to review the week. She hoped that by doing this she would be able to decide what was wrong with her class. A summary of her review follows:

Monday—Things went well. Students worked without serious disruptions. Carl, a really nice boy, brought a new game to school—*Aber, Aber, Aber.* None of the other children had seen the game before. They became quite excited. The only bad moment was when the game had to be put away. For a moment, Carl was quite angry. All in all, it was a good day. For a Monday, it was a very good day.

Tuesday—Things started fine. However, Wendy put a thumbtack on my chair during the third period. I punished her by not allowing her to play *Aber, Aber, Aber.* During the afternoon, someone placed a rotting onion in my center desk drawer. I saw Larry wandering around my desk earlier and thought about not letting him play *Aber, Aber, Aber.* I didn't do this.

Larry is too nice a boy to accuse just because he was near my desk. Tuesday was a bad day. I have never been happier to hear the dismissal bell for the day.

Wednesday—Things started bad and got no better. At the beginning, students refused to settle down and go to work. No matter what I tried I could not get them to attend to what they were supposed to do. Before the day was over, I found nasty comments about me written on the blackboard and on the bulletin board. I suspected Michael and Joan, but this made no sense to me. Michael and Joan are pleasant students. I have always thought that they liked me as a teacher.

Thursday—Carl was late. However, he was very polite as he handed me his tardy note. This made me feel good. I needed a boost. I thought, "Maybe things will go better today." But this was not to be. Again students did not work well. In addition, I had to break up a fight between Carl and Joan. It seems that Michael and Joan took Carl's new game home with them last night. The corner of the box in which the game is kept was torn. Carl accused Michael and Joan. But Carl and Joan said that Larry had done it the night before. After the fight, students were more restless than they had been before.

Ms. Phillips reviewed her notes. Suddenly, and to her surprise, she began to understand what had been happening in her fifth-grade class. Carl was controlling access to a new game that other children wanted to play.

She thought, ''He probably asked Wendy to put a thumbtack on my chair. He encouraged Larry to put an onion in my desk. He offered to let Michael and Joan take the game home for a night if they put remarks on the blackboard and bulletin board. It was Carl who disrupted the class for almost a whole week.''

Ms. Phillips has been hurt by the power of one of her students. This student, Carl, has the power to make teaching almost impossible for Ms. Phillips.

''Who would have thought it?'' Ms. Phillips smiled as she began to consider how she would handle the situation, now that she understood what had been happening.

COMPREHENSION

1. Who brings a new game to school?
2. When does Carl decide to hurt Ms. Phillips?
3. How does Carl hurt Ms. Phillips?
4. On one day, enough information becomes available for Ms. Phillips to know that Carl is the cause of her problems. Which day is this? How do you know Carl is at fault on this day?
5. How many students does Carl get to help him?
6. How many students does Carl hurt?

RELATIONAL

8. Carl can influence students like Larry, Michael, and Joan to behave in ways they do not wish to behave. This means he has power over them. What information in the story supports this?
9. Ms. Phillips will need to use power to influence Carl to behave as a student should behave. What can a teacher do in order to have power over the behavior of students?

VALUE/FEELING

10. How does Carl hurt his classmates in this story?
11. What should Ms. Phillips do about Wendy, Larry, Michael, and Joan? Explain your response.
12. What should Ms. Phillips do about Carl's behavior? Justify your response.

Hitch Your Wagon to a Job

Conceptual focus: Relative Deprivation

SOCIAL SITUATION

Rose and Carla wanted a wagon that they could ride. They rode their bicycles to the store. The cheapest wagon was $14.95. It was bright red and shiny white. It was just what they wanted.

Rose and Carla rode home. Each went to her house and counted her money. Carla had $2.55. Rose had $1.79. When they put their money together, they didn't have enough to buy the wagon.

Rose decided to see how much they still needed. She worked two problems:

$ 2.55	Carla has this much money.
1.79	I have this much money.
$ 4.34	We have this much money.

$14.95	What the wagon costs.
4.34	How much money we have.
$10.61	The money we need to buy the wagon.

Carla said, "Let's see if we can arrange to do some jobs. Maybe we can earn enough money to buy the wagon."

Rose said, "That's a good idea. Let's talk to some neighbors."

They went first to see Mrs. Pardo. Mrs. Pardo wanted to have her front yard raked.

She promised to pay the girls $1.50 to rake her front yard.

Mr. Smith wanted his lawn mowed. He offered to pay the girls $3.00 if they did a good job.

Mr. Washington offered to pay the girls $2.00 if they would clean his swimming pool.

Mrs. Camp wanted to have her car washed. She said she could only pay $1.00.

Rose's mother said, "I would like to have the outside of the windows washed. I can pay you and Carla $2.00."

Carla's mother also wanted to help Rose and Carla. She said, "The carport and utility room are a mess. If you clean them I will pay you $2.00."

Carla and Rose made a list of all these jobs. They wanted to see if they would have enough money to buy the new wagon. Their list looked like this:

$ 1.50	Mrs. Pardo	yard raked
3.00	Mr. Smith	lawn mowed
2.00	Mr. Washington	vacuum swimming pool
1.00	Mrs. Camp	car washed
2.00	Rose's mother	windows washed
2.00	Carla's mother	carport cleaned
$11.50		

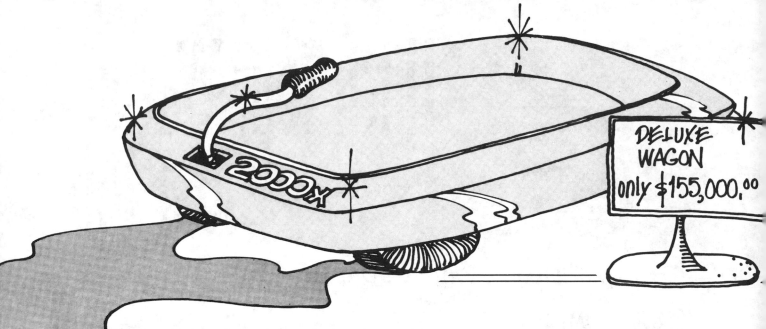

DELUXE WAGON only $155,000.00

Carla said, "Oh, boy!"

Rose said, "We'll have enough money, and we'll have almost a dollar left."

The girls worked hard for the next week. They raked Mrs. Pardo's yard, mowed Mr. Smith's lawn, cleaned Mr. Washington's swimming pool, and washed Mrs. Camp's car.

By Saturday morning, two jobs were left to be done. The windows must be washed for Rose's mother, and the carport must be done for Carla's mother. Rose and Carla were up bright and early. First, they did the windows. This took all morning.

After lunch they went to work on Carla's carport. By four o'clock they were finished.

Carla's mother said, "You girls have worked hard. I'll take you to get your new wagon."

When they reached the store, Rose and Carla were very excited. They rushed into the store. They quickly spotted the wagon they wanted.

Carla picked one up and said, "Let's go."

Carla's mother said, "Just a minute. Look at the price."

Rose looked at the sign. It was new. It read,

DELUXE WAGON only $16⁹⁵ !!

Carla said, "This can't be right. It's the same wagon we saw last Saturday. It's supposed to be $14.95."

Rose said, "That's right."

Carla's mother said, "Let's ask the store manager."

When they found the store manager he said, "I'm sorry. Last week the wagon cost $14.95. This week the wagon costs $16.95. All prices just keep going up and up."

Carla said, "That's a dirty trick."

Rose said, "This is not fair."

Both girls were disappointed. They counted up all their money. They had started with $4.34. They had earned $11.50. They didn't have enough money to pay the new price.

$ 4.34	Money to start with.
11.50	Money earned.
$15.84	All our money.

Both Carla and Rose were very unhappy. They had earned money to buy a wagon. While they were earning the money, the wagon became more costly. Both girls felt like crying.

Discussion Starters

COMPREHENSION
1. What did Rose and Carla want to buy?
2. How much money did the wagon cost?
3. How did the girls use their knowledge of mathematics?
4. How many tasks did Carla and Rose do to save up for the wagon?
5. In terms of being hurt, how much did wanting the wagon cost Rose and Carla?

RELATIONAL
6. Each time Rose and Carla finished a job, they were more able to buy the wagon. Their ability to buy was more like what they wanted it to be. This means that they were less and less *deprived* of what they wanted. What does being *less deprived* mean?
7. Rose and Carla went into the store believing they would leave with the new wagon. Because the wagon now cost more, they could not afford to buy it. Why did they want to cry this time but not the first time?

VALUE/FEELING
8. Suppose Carla's mother wants to help the two girls feel better. If she wants to help them, what should she do?
9. Suppose the store manager wants to help the two girls feel better. What should he do?
10. Suppose you were Rose or Carla. What would you do?

The Standard Format of the Value Sheet   41

SUDDEN WEALTH

Conceptual focus: Relative Deprivation

SOCIAL SITUATION

Ogma is a very small country located on the planet Oktu. Ogma has always been a poor country. It has always had very few good schools. There have not been enough hospitals to care for the ill.

For a long time, the people of Ogma have wanted to build enough good schools so that all children may be educated. Ogmans, for a long time, have also wanted to build more hospitals in order to care for the sick. Until last year, this seemed impossible.

Last year, a corporation found a major oil field located under Lake Ogma. The money from these oil reserves will increase the money available to those who govern Ogma.

Ogmans spoke confidently about using the money from oil to build more schools and hospitals—two goals they had wished but had not expected to achieve.

Ogmans were quite disappointed last week, though, when the Governor of Ogma spoke.

"My friends, I am aware that you expect my government to use money derived from the sale of our oil to build new schools and hospitals.

"I am sincerely sorry to disappoint you. Nevertheless, I must be honest with you. Our population is growing quite rapidly. This rapid population growth means that we will have to be more selective than we were in choosing who gets to go to school. This means that fewer of our ill will be able to secure hospital treatment."

Ogmans were very disappointed. Some groups talked about starting a revolution. In fact, the Ogmans felt that they had been deprived and cheated. The Ogmans were suffering from a condition of relative deprivation.

In this case, the expectations of the Ogmans—to have more schools and hospitals—increase. The capability that Ogmans have for securing more schools and hospitals decreases because of rapid population growth. Whenever the expectations of a person or group increase and the abilities of a person or group to attain these expectations decline, a condition of *relative deprivation* occurs.

Discussion Starters

COMPREHENSION

1. Where does this story take place?
2. What are some of the things that Ogmans want?
3. What makes Ogmans believe they can have more good things than they used to have?
4. Ogmans are told that they cannot have the good things they expect to have. Why?

RELATIONAL

5. If expectations grow faster than a group's ability to have the good things members of the group expect, persons are likely to feel deprived. Is this statement true for this story? (Be prepared to explain your response.)
6. If a group expects more than it can have for a long time, the group is likely to feel deprived. Describe at least one situation in which you have been deprived.

VALUE/FEELING

7. Should the Ogmans start a revolution?
8. The governor said, ''I must be honest with you.'' Assume the governor wishes to remain in power. If this is true, did the governor do the right thing?
9. Pretend you are the ruler of the Ogmans. If you were, how would you try to help them feel better?
10. The governor says that population growth is costing Ogmans a chance for good schools and good health care. Should those who rule or govern force citizens to control population growth? Defend your response.

The Standard Format of the Value Sheet   43

From the Teacher's Perspective ⸺

The standard format of the value sheet may also be thought of in terms of how it may be utilized. In using a standard format of the value sheet, assign the value sheet and (1) remind students of the topic, concept, or idea that is currently being studied; (2) inform students that the stimulus situation is relevant to the current focus of study; and (3) indicate that once students have had an opportunity to study the social situation, they will be expected to respond, personally and publicly, to directions and questions.

Next, allow students a period of time in which to study the resource. This should be a quiet time in which no talking and no excess movement occurs. Here, you must be especially alert; for it is the teacher who is most likely to disrupt student attention by talking, moving about, or engaging in some other distracting activity. The importance of this period of quiet study will be emphasized for each of the five formats of the value sheet presented.

When students have studied the resource, distribute the discussion starters and ask students individually to write answers to these questions and directions. Discussion starters are not distributed prior to the time that students have studied the social situation, to keep them from just looking for answers to the discussion starters. When students are writing initial reactions to the discussion starters, it is important that they work alone.

Once students have written responses to the discussion starters, use these questions and directions as a basis to ascertain that students have (1) comprehended the social situation; (2) framed relationships between the social situation and the current focus of study; and (3) reacted personally in terms of their values and feelings toward the social situation. You may not use all the questions found in the discussion starters, and you are almost certain to use questions not found in the discussion starters. It is also unlikely that you will use the questions found in the discussion starters in the same order as they are written. Your role at this stage is to provide for comprehension, analysis, and personalization, doing whatever is necessary to secure these instructional ends.

Finally, summarize what you believe students have

learned by reacting to the value sheet and proceed to introduce the next learning activity that they are to use.

Each of these five phases of usage are important. The initial assignment tends to focus student attention and establish a learning set. The study time creates optimum conditions for students to acquire and begin to process information. Asking students to write answers enhances the likelihood that they will participate in the discussion that follows. The discussion of individual student responses enables students to contrast how they have reasoned with how other students have reasoned and provides both the teacher and other students with the chance to challenge students to think in new ways. The teacher summary at the end helps students to isolate those aspects of the learning activity that are worthy of being remembered and/or used.

On Your Own

Most standard instructional resources may be converted into standard format value sheets. To accomplish this, take the following steps:

1. Define or delimit the focus of study within which you intend to use the value sheet.
2. Select a reading, a visual or audio resource that is relevant to the current focus of study in your class. Alternatively, you may choose to paraphrase such a resource or write your own social situation.
3. Write four, five, or six questions that students may use in order to test their understanding of the social situation. (Conventions for doing this were presented above in the section entitled "Description.")
4. Write two, three, or four relational questions that will help students seek out relationships between the social situation and their current focus of study. (Conventions for doing this have been presented, above.)
5. Write two to five value/feeling questions that will require students to express personal preferences and feelings about the social situation. (See the conventions for doing this, above.)

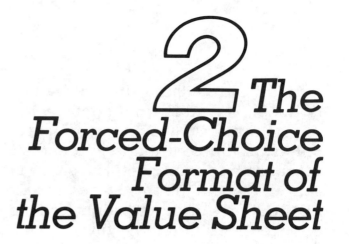

2 The Forced-Choice Format of the Value Sheet

Functions

When an individual or group needs to make a decision between two courses of action, one good and one bad, it is seldom difficult to do so. Many important decisions, however, are not of this type. Individuals and members of groups frequently find themselves in decision-making situations where they must choose the greater good at the expense of sacrificing other good things; or, they find themselves in decision-making situations where they must opt for the lesser evil as the price to be paid in order to avoid actions that are even worse. *As it is structured, the forced-choice format of the value sheet provides situations in which students, as individuals and as members of a group, seek the greater good or the lesser evil.*

Description

The forced-choice format of the value sheet contains four components: a social context, a list of options, an individual decision sheet, and a group decision sheet. Each of these components will be described.

The social situation confronts students with a situation within which an individual or a group must make a decision from a limited number of options; hence the name, forced-choice. The social situation establishes the constraints within which a decision is to be made. Here, it is also desirable to provide sufficient information for students to assume the roles of persons who are presented in the social situation, i.e., to engage in role-taking.

The second component is a short list of options, usually three to five in number. These are the only policies that students are to consider in order to make an appropriate decision for the social situation provided. These options are homogeneous. All of the options are either positive or negative. This, in effect, structures a situation in which students must choose the greater good at the price of sacrificing other good options; or, students must choose the lesser evil in order to avoid other and worse options.

The third component is an individual decision sheet. This is to be completed by students working independently and prior to any group effort to discuss the relative merits of the different options. This decision sheet elicits two forms of student behavior. First, each student selects the option that he believes is best for the situation given. Second, each student explains why he believes that the option selected is best. Once this decision sheet has been completed, individual student reactions are available and are likely to become an integral component of the value clarification exercise.

The fourth component is a group decision sheet. Groups of four or five students work together in order to complete this decision sheet. The group decision sheet is intended to cue three forms of student behavior. Students share their individual reactions with one another and re-examine the social situation at the focus of the activity. They use communication and persuasion skills in order to seek consensus with regard to one decision and one rationale that they, as a group, are willing to share with other members of the class.

Classroom Examples

Five examples of the forced-choice format of the value sheet are provided here. Study at least four of these examples in order to develop the understanding necessary to use or write your own value sheets written in this format.

A Visitor in Limestone

Conceptual focus: Conflict

SOCIAL SITUATION

Mayor Carson has been mayor of Limestone for more than fifteen years. Limestone is a beautiful little town. It is located in a high valley in the mountains of the Northwest. It is surrounded on all sides by a beautiful forest. A sparkling clear river full of fish runs by the town.

Limestone has a small population. Each year more people leave because there are few jobs. Besides, jobs in the cities pay more money. Limestone has many empty buildings. Some people say, "The town of Limestone is dying."

Mayor Carson hates to see her town become smaller and smaller. She knows that she needs to find some way to keep people from moving away.

Yesterday, Mayor Carson found one possible answer. A man who works for a company that makes clothes came to see Mayor Carson. The visitor said, "My company wants to build a factory in Limestone. Our factory will make shirts and socks. We will hire local people to work in this factory."

There is one big problem. While making socks and shirts, the new factory will produce waste products. The company wants to dump these waste products into the river. If they do this, the water will become cloudy and dirty, and many of the fish will be killed.

Mayor Carson is undecided. She wants the factory because the people of Limestone need jobs. She wants to protect the river because it is one of the things that makes Limestone a fine place to live. Mayor Carson very much wants both of these things. Her two wishes are in conflict.

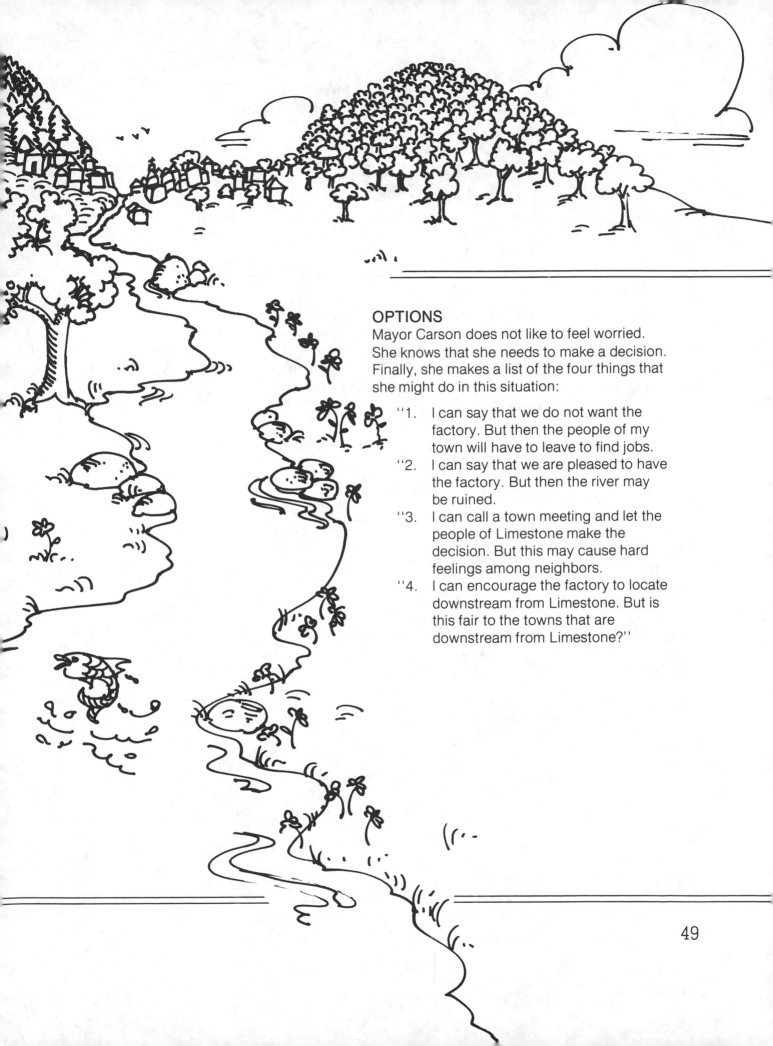

OPTIONS

Mayor Carson does not like to feel worried. She knows that she needs to make a decision. Finally, she makes a list of the four things that she might do in this situation:

"1. I can say that we do not want the factory. But then the people of my town will have to leave to find jobs.

"2. I can say that we are pleased to have the factory. But then the river may be ruined.

"3. I can call a town meeting and let the people of Limestone make the decision. But this may cause hard feelings among neighbors.

"4. I can encourage the factory to locate downstream from Limestone. But is this fair to the towns that are downstream from Limestone?"

Individual Decision Sheet

Use this decision sheet to record what you would do if you were Mayor Carson. Complete this decision sheet by yourself. Do not discuss it with anyone until you have completed it.

Select the *best* thing that Mayor Carson can do in this situation. Indicate your choice by using a check mark (✓).

_____ Tell the visitor that you do not want the factory.
_____ Tell the visitor that you want the factory.
_____ Call a town meeting and let the people decide.
_____ Ask the visitor to locate the factory downstream.

I believe my answer is best, because: _____
_____
_____
_____
_____
_____
_____

From J. Doyle Casteel, *Learning to Think and Choose.* © 1978 Goodyear Publishing Company, Inc. Santa Monica, CA 90401

Group Decision Sheet

Imagine that you and the other members of your group are the town council of Limestone. Mayor Carson has asked your group to decide what she should do as Mayor. Try to agree on one answer without voting.

As a group, we believe the mayor should

_____ welcome the new factory.

_____ oppose the new factory.

_____ call a town meeting.

_____ try to locate the factory downstream.

We believe our recommendation is best, because: _____
_____
_____
_____
_____
_____
_____
_____

Members making this decision are: _____
_____
_____
_____
_____
_____

From J. Doyle Casteel, *Learning to Think and Choose,* © 1978 Goodyear Publishing Company, Inc. Santa Monica, CA 90401

Two Men of High Honor

Conceptual focus: Cooperation

SOCIAL SITUATION

For purposes of this exercise, you are to imagine that you are a Baptist preacher. You have just become the new preacher at the Milltown Baptist Church. Right away, you find that some men are doing evil things. You want to stop these men from doing the bad things they are doing in Milltown.

Milltown is located near the Smokey Mountains. It serves the needs of farmers and mill workers.

Milltown is a very small town. There is one service station where one may buy gas and oil. There is one drugstore where one may buy drugs. There are two stores where one may buy clothing, food, and other items. These are called general stores.

Most of the people who live in Milltown are very poor. Most of those who live in town work in a mill where paper is made. They are not paid very well. They almost never get a raise. These workers cannot afford to go to the city to buy their clothes and food, and the nearest large town is 150 miles away over poor roads.

The farmers who live in the country around Milltown are also quite poor. Their farms are rocky and hilly, but they do sell one crop for money—this cash crop is tobacco.

Besides tobacco, these farmers grow much of their own food. Like the poor people who live in Milltown itself, the farmers cannot afford to go to the city to buy food and clothing.

Mr. Fred and Mr. Roy own the two general stores which offer food and clothing for sale. Mr. Fred's store is at the north end of Milltown. It is called the Northside General Store.

Mr. Roy's store is located at the south end of Milltown. It is called the Milltown General Store.

Mr. Fred and Mr. Roy are important people in Milltown. Mr. Fred is the mayor of the town. Mr. Roy is a member of the school board. Each man wants to be a good citizen.

Mr. Fred and Mr. Roy go to the same church, the one in which you preach. They are both leaders in the church. Both teach Sunday school classes. Both are deacons. Each man wants to be a good Christian.

Mr. Fred and Mr. Roy are both members of the Milltown Leadership Club. The Leadership Club is the most important group in Milltown. The men who manage the paper-mill factory are members. The men who own the business places in Milltown are members. The school principal and the school superintendent are members. Mr. Fred and Mr. Roy are proud to be members of the Milltown Leadership Club.

Mr. Fred and Mr. Roy make good money in their stores. Most of the men and women who work in the paper mill buy their food and clothes from Mr. Fred or Mr. Roy.

Years ago, Mr. Fred and Mr. Roy agreed that they would always do certain things. Among these were the following:

"1. We will never have special prices on household goods. Sugar, coffee, salt, bread, flour, meal, shortening, and spices will cost the same all six days of the week.

"2. We will never have weekend special prices for hamburger meat, steaks, hams, turkeys, or chickens. All meat will be the same price six days of the week.

"3. We will never put work shoes, work clothes, coats, or other clothing on sale. All our customers will always pay the full price for such goods.

"4. We will never give stamps to customers who shop with us. We could pass part of this cost on to our customers. However, since we would have to pay part of the cost, this would cut down on the profits we want to make.

53

"5. Each time we cash a weekly payroll check or a social security check we will charge fifty cents. However, neither of us will charge our friends or members of the Leadership Club for this service. Only workers and farmers will be charged."

These rules mean that the millworkers and the poor farmers must pay more for their food, clothing, and supplies. These rules mean that Mr. Fred and Mr. Roy will make more money. These rules also mean that some children may go hungry and cold.

Mr. Fred and Mr. Roy have never signed an agreement. They trust one another and have cooperated with one another for a long time. They have made good money.

One day when Mr. Fred was talking to Mr. Roy, Mr. Roy said, "Shucks, Mr. Fred, we don't need to sign anything. We're both honorable men and civic leaders."

Mr. Fred responded. "I agree. Good Christians like us will always keep our word and be good men."

When you, as the new Baptist preacher, became aware of how Mr. Fred and Mr. Roy did business, you were shocked. You really believe that each person should treat all others as he would wish to be treated. You feel that you must do something to keep Mr. Fred and Mr. Roy from mistreating the poor workers and farmers.

At the same time, you know that Mr. Fred and Mr. Roy are important members of your church. Were they to leave, your church would lose their weekly offering. The loss of this money would hurt the church. Finally, you make a list of four things that you might do. From this list of four possibilities, you intend to choose one. This list of options appears below.

OPTIONS
1. Preach a sermon on the evil of greed and the virtue of charity.
2. Condemn Mr. Fred and Mr. Roy in a sermon next Sunday and ask them to change their rules.
3. Talk to Mr. Roy and Mr. Fred privately but do nothing to embarrass them publicly.
4. Organize the millworkers and help them start their own general store.

Individual Decision Sheet

Use this decision sheet to record what you would do if you were the new Baptist minister. Complete this decision sheet by yourself. Do not discuss it with anyone until you have completed it.

Select the best thing that you, as the Baptist minister, can do in this situation. Indicate your choice with a check mark (✓).

_____ Preach a sermon. Stress the need to be good citizens.

_____ Preach a sermon. Condemn Mr. Fred's and Mr. Roy's actions.

_____ Just talk to Mr. Fred and Mr. Roy. Don't say anything publicly.

_____ Help the millworkers start their own general store.

Suppose you were asked by another minister to defend your choice. How would you convince him that your choice is best?

I would say _____

_____

_____

_____

_____

_____

_____

_____

From J. Doyle Casteel, *Learning to Think and Choose*, © 1978 Goodyear Publishing Company, Inc. Santa Monica, CA 90401

Group Decision Sheet Directions

In order to respond to this decision sheet, all members of your group must pretend that a number of things are true.

- ○ All members of your group attend the new minister's church. He has asked you to help him decide what he should do.
- ○ All members of your group like the new minister. You want him to do well in your town.
- ○ All members of your group believe in the golden rule.
- ○ All members of your group believe that the church needs the money that Mr. Fred and Mr. Roy give each Sunday.
- ○ All members of your group believe that Mr. Fred and Mr. Roy are cooperating to do a bad thing.
- ○ All members of your group want your church to be a good church. You want the church to help all the people who live in or shop in Milltown.

Keep these things in mind as you complete this decision sheet. Also, keep in mind that you are to agree to the *one* best thing that the minister can do. Try to agree without voting.

From J. Doyle Casteel, *Learning to Think and Choose,* © 1978 Goodyear Publishing Company, Inc. Santa Monica, CA 90401

Group Decision Sheet

We believe that the best thing our preacher can do is to

_____ preach a sermon telling people it is wrong to be greedy. Tell people it is good to be kind and help the poor.

_____ preach a sermon telling people the kinds of rules Mr. Fred and Mr. Roy use to make a good profit. Tell people that Mr. Fred and Mr. Roy should stop doing these bad things.

_____ talk to Mr. Fred and Mr. Roy but do not make them mad. The church needs their money.

_____ start a new store telling people that Milltown needs a store that is run by persons who want to help the poor.

We believe our choice is best, because: _____

_____
_____
_____
_____
_____
_____

Members participating in this decision are: _____

_____
_____
_____
_____
_____

From J. Doyle Casteel, *Learning to Think and Choose,* © 1978 Goodyear Publishing Company, Inc. Santa Monica, CA 90401

HOMECOMING

SOCIAL SITUATION

Mascot has always been a small town. The people who live in the country around Mascot are truck farmers. They raise vegetables and take them to the city about sixty miles away. They sell most of their vegetables to grocery stores located in the city.

Mascot has a large hardware store. The hardware store sells tools, fertilizer, and home repair items. It also sells electric stoves, refrigerators, and television sets.

Mascot has one service station. The owner of the service station is also a mechanic. He fixes cars, tractors, and trucks.

Mascot also has one grocery store. In addition to food the store also sells work clothes and shoes.

Unless the people of Mascot can find what they want in these stores, they must go to the city to shop.

Recently, a man who grew up in Mascot returned home. His name is Mr. Willy.

Mr. Willy moved to the city when he was twenty-five years old. For the last twenty years, he has worked for a television store in the city as a television repairman.

Soon after returning to Mascot, Mr. Willy told his friends he was going to start a new store. "I will sell refrigerators, freezers, stoves, air conditioners, radios, stereos, CBs, and television sets. With my training, I will be able to service what I sell. I believe the town of Mascot needs a store whose only business is appliances."

When Mr. Schmidt, who owns the hardware store, was told, he was surprised. "Imagine that," he said.

"What will you do, Mr. Schmidt?" he was asked.

"We'll see," Mr. Schmidt answered.

Mr. Schmidt thought of several things he might do when Mr. Willy opened his new store. The things Mr. Schmidt began to think about are the options that follow.

OPTIONS

"I might sell appliances for just what they cost me. Then, Mr. Willy could make no profit. Soon he would have to close his store. Then, I could raise the cost of my appliances and make a good profit.

"I might ask Mr. Willy to buy my stock of appliances. Who knows? What I sell may be more trouble than it is worth. If I sell my stock to Mr. Willy, I can put my effort into selling hardware goods and services.

"I might hire a serviceman to work in my hardware store. This will enable me to offer the same services Mr. Willy will offer. Since my business is established, Mr. Willy will probably make too little money to stay in business.

"My customers depend on me for tools, seed, and fertilizer. Many of them buy these things on credit and then pay me when they sell the first of their crops. They even borrow money from me in emergencies. I'll let these people know that I expect them to be loyal customers. If I catch them buying from Mr. Willy, I'll make it tough for them."

Individual Decision Sheet

Complete this decision sheet before you discuss it with other members of your class. Select the one thing you would do if you were Mr. Schmidt. Mark your choice with a check mark (✓).

_____ Sell my goods at cost and drive Mr. Willy out of business.
_____ Try to sell my appliances to Mr. Willy.
_____ Hire a serviceman to work in the hardware store.
_____ Force my customers to be loyal to me.

As Mr. Schmidt, I believe my choice is best because:

_____
_____
_____
_____
_____
_____
_____

From J. Doyle Castel, *Learning to Think and Choose.* © 1978 Goodyear Publishing Company, Inc. Santa Monica, CA 90401

Group Decision Sheet

Work with members of your group in order to complete this exercise. As a group select the one best policy that Mr. Schmidt should use. Try to reach agreement without voting. When you have finished you will be allowed to share the decision your group makes with other members of the class.

We believe Mr. Schmidt should
_____ sell his goods at cost and drive Mr. Willy out of business.
_____ sell his appliances to Mr. Willy.
_____ hire his own serviceman.
_____ force customers who owe him favors to do business at his hardware store.

If asked to defend our choice, we would say

_____
_____
_____
_____
_____
_____

Group members responsible for this decision are: _____
_____
_____
_____
_____

On Cheating and Being Fair

Conceptual focus: Power

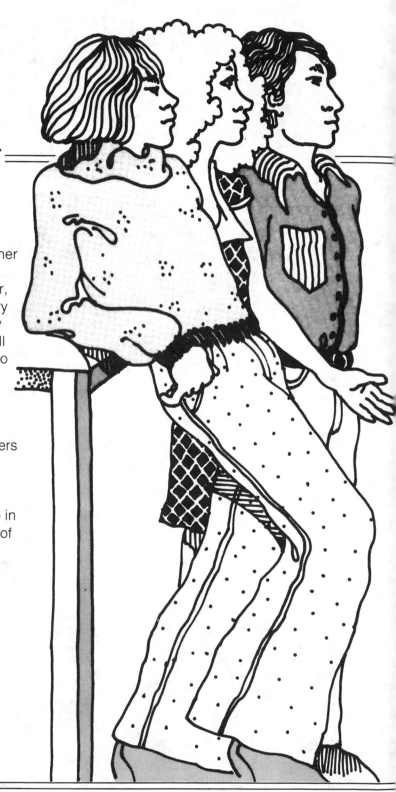

SOCIAL SITUATION

Last Friday, Mrs. Johnson was unable to teach her eighth-grade American history class. The principal called a substitute teacher who took Mrs. Johnson's place.

Mrs. Johnson told the substitute teacher, "You should have an easy day. Almost every Friday I ask students to respond to a weekly quiz. This helps my students to see how well they are learning American History. This also helps me to plan what I will do as teacher."

The substitute teacher did as Mrs. Johnson had asked her to do. She had students respond to a weekly quiz.

Today, Mrs. Johnson graded all the papers for her fifth-period American history class. After grading the papers, Mrs. Johnson is certain that four of her students cheated.

Mrs. Johnson does not know what to do in this situation. She has thought of a number of things she might do, and these are listed below as options.

OPTIONS

○ Mrs. Johnson might offer to reward anyone who tells her how the four students cheated.

○ Mrs. Johnson might throw all the papers away. She could tell her fifth-period students the papers are lost and give them another test.

○ Mrs. Johnson might tell her fifth-period class she believes a number of students cheated. She could then refuse to record any of the grades in her record book.

○ Mrs. Johnson might keep all members of the class after school. She could give them a grade of zero. This would set an example for all her students.

○ Mrs. Johnson might say nothing and record the grades. Then in the future she can avoid asking a substitute teacher to give tests in her classes.

Individual Decision Sheet

Suppose that you really like and respect Mrs. Johnson. Suppose also that she asks you to advise her. Given these two conditions, complete this decision sheet. Do this by yourself.

Of the five options that follow, Mrs. Johnson should
_____ pretend that all papers have been lost.
_____ refuse to record any of the grades.
_____ keep the entire class after school.
_____ record all grades and say nothing else.
_____ offer to reward an informer.

If asked to justify my advice, I would use the following defense:_____
_____
_____
_____
_____
_____
_____

From J. Doyle Casteel, *Learning to Think and Choose*, © 1978 Goodyear Publishing Company, Inc. Santa Monica, CA 90401

Group Decision Sheet

Work with other members of your group in order to complete this decision sheet. Try to reach an agreement as to what Mrs. Johnson should do. Do not vote.

We believe Mrs. Johnson should
_____ pretend that all the papers have been lost.
_____ refuse to record any of the grades.
_____ keep the entire class after school.
_____ record all grades and say nothing to the class.
_____ offer to reward an informer.

We believe this choice is best for the following reasons:
_____
_____
_____
_____
_____
_____
_____

Persons responsible for this decision are: _____
_____
_____
_____
_____

From J. Doyle Casteel, *Learning to Think and Choose.* © 1978 Goodyear Publishing Company, Inc. Santa Monica, CA 90401

BOUNCING AROUND

Conceptual focus: Relative Deprivation

SOCIAL SITUATION

Leah loved sports. She especially loved to play basketball.

Leah was not a good athlete. She was not fast, she did not shoot basketballs very well, and she did not run fast.

In sixth grade, Leah went out for the basketball team. She barely made the team. Most of the time she sat on the bench and watched other girls play.

Leah decided she would work hard. All summer she practiced. She practiced bouncing, passing, and shooting basketballs. She practiced running sideways and backwards so she could play better defense. She wanted to be able to play defense as well as to help her team score points.

When the next season arrived, Leah tried out for the seventh-grade basketball team. She was sure she would be first string.

However, the other girls had also improved. They ran faster, shot better, and passed the ball and played defense with more skill. Although Leah was improved, the other girls with more ability had improved even more rapidly than she.

The coach came to Leah and said, "I know how hard you have worked and how much you have improved. I want to keep you on the team but you'll seldom get to play. You'll spend nearly all your time on the bench."

Leah just barely held back her tears.

The coach continued, "I know you must be very disappointed. I will understand if you want to call it quits."

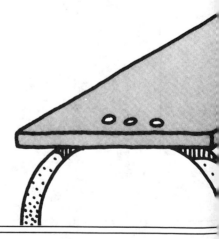

OPTIONS

Leah could think of only three things that she might do. These were:

1. To quit the team and do something else.
2. To stay on the team and accept that she will not get to play.
3. To stay on the team and hope the coach changes her mind.

Individual
Decision
Sheet

Work by yourself to complete this decision sheet. Later, you will have an opportunity to share your work with other members of a small group. As you answer, pretend that you are Leah and want to play basketball very much.

My three choices are (use your own words):

1. _____
2. _____
3. _____

Of these three choices, the best thing I can do in this situation is_____
_____
_____
_____
_____
_____
_____
_____

I believe this is my best choice because
_____
_____
_____
_____
_____
_____

From J. Doyle Casteel, *Learning to Think and Choose*, © 1978 Goodyear Publishing Company, Inc. Santa Monica, CA 90401

Group
Decision
Sheet

Work together on this assignment. First, find out how each member of your group responded to the individual decision sheet. Then try to agree as a group on the best choice that Leah might make. Afterwards, you will be expected to share your decision with other members of the class.

We believe that Leah should _____

_____

_____

_____

_____

_____

We believe that this is the best choice for Leah for the following reasons:

_____

_____

_____

_____

_____

_____

Group members making this decision are: _____

_____

_____

_____

_____

From the Teacher's Perspective ========

When using a forced-choice format of the value sheet, initiate the activity by reviewing the current focus of study—the topic, theme, concept, or idea that is being studied. Then proceed by indicating that the value clarification activity students will be reacting to is related to the current focus of study. Also indicate that individuals and groups must sometimes choose the greater good or the lesser evil. Behaviors such as these tend to establish a learning set according to which students perceive purpose in what they are asked to do.

With a learning set established, distribute the social situation and the limited list of options. Ask students to study the situation and the list of options carefully; also tell them that they will need to comprehend these two components because such understanding is critical to the completion of the activity.

Then give the students a period of time in which to study the social situation and the list of options. During this period of study time you should maintain a learning environment in which there is no unnecessary movement or talk. Although this point was stressed in Chapter 1, it is important to note again that you must act as your own watchdog in order to avoid one of the prime sources of disruptive behavior.

Once students have studied the social situation, ascertain that they have comprehended it and can relate it to the current focus of study. In order to do this, use comprehension and relational directions and questions phrased according to the conventions presented in Chapter 1. At this point, discourage any effort that students might make to express judgmental statements about the limited set of options.

Next, distribute the individual decision sheet. Tell students that they are to complete this decision sheet prior to discussing it with other students, and that once they have completed it, they will have a chance to share opinions with other members of a small group.

When students have completed the individual decision sheet, place them into small decision-making groups. It is important here to obtain a good mix of students that cuts across informal classroom groups and cliques. To do this, randomly select a student and then assign all students a number by counting off: "one," "two," "three," "four," and "five." Continue to do this until each student has been assigned a number. All students assigned a number—for example, the number "one "—become a group.

Prior to the time that students move into small groups to complete the group decision sheet, explain the assignment. Stress that students are to begin by sharing individual reactions and then to seek consensus. This explanation helps to curtail confusion and unnecessary noise.

The students who are organized into small groups begin by sharing their individual reactions to the social situation. With this accomplished, students seek consensus with regard to the best option and a rationale for this selection. During this period of interaction you should move about the room, quietly monitoring student performance. Monitor each group with at least four questions in mind:

1. Are all members of the group participating?
2. Do members of the group share personal reactions?
3. Do members of the group seek consensus with regard to the best option?
4. Do members of the group seek consensus with regard to the best criterion or explanation for the option they select as best?

Using these questions, intervene if necessary. On the other hand, avoid becoming a party to group discussions whenever you judge them to be functioning successfully.

Then, close the activity by doing at least two things. First, ask one member of each group to share that group's work with other members of the class. Second, review with students some of the important ways in which the value clarification activity is relevant to the current focus of study in the class where the value sheet has been used.

On Your Own

In order to develop your own examples of the forced-choice format of the value sheet, take the following steps:

1. State your current focus of study clearly.
2. Locate or develop a social situation relevant to your current focus of study in which an individual or group must make a decision.
3. Write comprehension and relational discussion starters that you can use in order to help students read and analyze the social situation.
4. Frame and state three to five possible reactions to this social situation.
5. Make sure the reactions listed are homogeneous.
6. Ascertain that these reactions tend to be good options or bad options so that students are confronted with either choosing the greater good or the lesser evil.
7. Develop an individual decision sheet that cues student behavior and provides a record of personal reactions.
8. Develop a group decision sheet that cues group behavior and provides a record of conclusions agreed to by the members of each group.

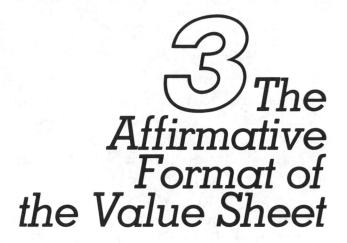

3 The Affirmative Format of the Value Sheet

Functions

The affirmative format is structured to yield at least five types of student value clarification behavior: (1) each student is confronted with a social situation that requires resolution and is asked to list possible courses of action that might be used in order to resolve the problem presented; (2) from the list of alternatives developed, each student selects the procedure that is most likely to resolve the social situation given; (3) each student identifies a criterion that might be employed in order to justify the alternative selected for use in the social situation; (4) students, organized in small groups, share the alternatives each student has identified for resolving the situation and his criterion; and (5) each group seeks consensus with regard to what ought to be done in order to resolve the social situation and establishes a rationale supportive of this position. This group work is then shared with members of other groups.

The affirmative format differs from the forced-choice format in that students are required to develop their own list of options. Whereas the forced-choice format tends to stress that in making decisions, one must often choose the greater good or the lesser evil, the affirmative format emphasizes that actors in a decision-making situation must often initiate their work by developing a range of alternatives.

Description

The affirmative format of the value sheet contains three components. There is a short story in which an individual or group encounters a problem that demands a decision. There is an individual decision sheet that both cues and structures the reactions of each student. And there is a group decision sheet that helps members of small groups to share individual reactions as well as seek agreement with regard to both a policy to be adopted and a rationale according to which this decision may be made reasonable to other class members. In other words, the affirmative value sheet is so structured as to secure student behaviors congruent with its function.

Classroom Examples

Five affirmative format examples of the value sheet are provided here. To enhance your understanding of the components of this format of the value sheet and of the student behaviors that are likely to be stimulated by this type of value clarification exercise, study at least four of the five examples presented. Such understanding, in turn, will help you consider one approach you may adopt in order to use this format of the value sheet.

Conceptual focus: Conflict

SOCIAL SITUATION

Lydia Spitz is attending Nob Hill Middle School for the first time. As a new seventh grader, she needs to make friends.

Quickly, Lydia decides that she would like to be friends with Connie and Juanita. Both are attractive girls who get along well with other students. Both are leaders in all types of classroom activities.

Because Lydia wants to become friends with Connie and Juanita, she is very happy when Connie invites her to a Halloween party. This will be Lydia's chance to build a good friendship.

When Lydia arrived at Connie's house for the Halloween party, she promised herself, "I will show them that I can be a good and loyal member of their group. I will make them want to be my friends just as much as I want to be their friend."

At first, the party went well. The games were fun, there were many refreshments, and everyone was friendly.

Then Connie and Juanita approached Lydia, who was talking with some other people at the party. They said, "Come on, Lydia. Let's take a walk and get some fresh air."

Once outside, Connie took a cigarette from her purse. Juanita said, "Lydia, we really like you. This is our way of asking you to be best friends with us. We want you to share our cigarette with us."

Lydia is very confused. If she smokes, she will do something she believes is wrong. She believes smoking is wrong because it is unhealthy, because she has promised her parents that she will not smoke, and because it is a habit that costs a lot of money. For all these reasons, Lydia wants to answer with a loud, "No way!"

At the same time, Lydia wants to accept Juanita's offer. She knows that sharing just one cigarette will not hurt her body. She knows that sharing just one cigarette is something her parents are unlikely to discover, and will cost her no money. If she refuses, she may never have another chance to become good friends with Juanita and Connie. For all these reasons, Lydia very much wants to answer with a loud, "You bet!"

Lydia wants to share the cigarette. Lydia also wants to refuse to share the cigarette. But she cannot do both. If she shares the cigarette, she cannot refuse to smoke. If she smokes, she cannot refuse to share the cigarette. These two desires are in conflict with one another. Because these two desires are in conflict, Lydia feels very confused.

Now, pretend that you are Lydia Spitz. As Lydia Spitz, you want to do the very best thing that you can do in this situation. Use the first decision sheet to guide and record your work.

Individual Decision Sheet

Complete this decision sheet by yourself. Do not discuss it with other members of the class until you have finished. Later, you will have an opportunity to share your work with other members of a small group.

Pretend that you are Lydia Spitz. List at least four things that you might do in this situation:

A. I might _____

_____

_____

B. I might _____

_____

_____

C. I might _____

_____

_____

D. I might _____

_____

_____

The best thing that I might do in this situation is to _____

_____

_____

Suppose someone said your decision was ridiculous. If this happened, defend your choice as best because _____

_____

_____

_____

From J. Doyle Casteel, *Learning to Think and Choose.* © 1978 Goodyear Publishing Company, Inc. Santa Monica, CA 90401

Group Decision Sheet

Work with other members of your group to complete this decision sheet. Later, a member of your group will be asked to share the decisions made by your group with other members of the class.

List the things that each member of the group believes Lydia should do in this situation:

A. _____
_____

B. _____
_____

C. _____
_____

D. _____
_____

E. _____
_____

As a group, agree on the single best thing that Lydia can and should do. You may select one of the recommendations made by an individual member of your group. Or, you may find another alternative. We believe the best thing Lydia can do is to_____
_____
_____

If questioned, we would justify our choice by saying_____
_____
_____

Members participating in this group are: _____
_____
_____
_____

From J. Doyle Casteel, *Learning to Think and Choose,* © 1978 Goodyear Publishing Company, Inc. Santa Monica, CA 90401

An Invitation to Dinner
New Adventures with a New Company

Conceptual focus: Cooperation

SOCIAL SITUATION

The time is 1617. The place is London, England.

A group of ten shipowners are eating dinner together. They are also talking about their businesses. You are one of these people. In fact, you have been asked to eat with the other nine owners for the first time today.

You are proud of your invitation to have dinner with the other shipowners. They are wise people and sharp traders.

In addition, you feel honored. You have worked hard for a long time. You have saved your money and have used your money wisely in order to make more money. You have earned the right to sit and eat and exchange trade secrets with these other wealthy people. Exchanging trade secrets with them will help you to make more money. Your invitation to have dinner with the other shipowners is only fair. It tells you that you have been a successful person.

And you are a wealthy man. You own a fleet of seven ships. You have ships that carry cargoes from India and the Far East to England. You have ships that sail the West Coast of Africa dodging the Portuguese and seeking trade. You have ships that carry goods made in England to Italy, Greece, and the Middle East. You are proud that you are a rich and powerful man. You want to continue to work and hope to become even richer. In fact, you believe you must continue to work and earn more money. It is a duty that you owe to your God. And owing the debt to God, you also owe it to yourself.

You are also a Christian. Although you attend Church of England services, you are really a Puritan. You are called a Puritan because you want to purify the Church of England. You want to make it a church that is really Christian. You are pleased to know that the people with whom you are eating are also Christians and Puritans.

You believe that all men were created by God. Because all men were created by God, you also believe that all men are important. The life of every single person is important.

One of your new friends, Mr. Horn, is talking. Mr. Horn says, "Yesterday I talked with a man from our colony in Virginia. This man said that Virginia is a rich land. He also said that there are not enough workers to develop the riches of the colony. He said that Englishmen in America would pay good money for servants."

Mr. Horn paused, took a sip of wine, and allowed his words to sink in. He obviously had gained his friends' attention when he talked about good money. Then, Mr. Horn continued.

"This started me to thinking. The Spanish buy black men in Africa. They then take these black men to Spanish America where they work as slaves. Sir Francis Drake and Sir John Hawkins made good money buying and selling slaves a few years ago. We, too, might earn a handsome profit in this way.

"We could trade for blacks along the West Coast of Africa. We could take the slaves to the American colony. We could exchange the slaves for raw materials and bring the raw materials back to England and sell them. This should give us a good profit. I don't see how we could lose."

A second man, Mr. Winth, interrupted Mr. Horn. "I don't know, Mr. Horn. But I have some doubts. None of us have ever traded in slaves before. It is true that we might make good profits. On the other hand, we might lose a great deal of money.

"To do something new is always dangerous. If we weren't making good money, it might be worth taking a chance. But we are making good money. I am not sure we should risk the good profits we are making in order to try and increase our earnings."

Mr. Winth ended his comments by saying, "I'm not sure, Mr. Horn. I am willing to listen further. But I have my doubts about the new venture."

Mr. Horn answered Mr. Winth. "What you say is true, Mr. Winth. We are making good money. To trade in slaves would be a new adventure for us. And to do new things means one must accept risks. Perhaps we should forget the matter for now."

At this point, Mr. Smithe began to speak. "Gentlemen, I find myself agreeing with both of you. I agree with Mr. Horn. To buy slaves in Africa and sell them in America is a way that we can earn good profits. It is our duty to make money, to use what God has given us wisely at all times. I also agree with Mr. Winth. This is a new type of adventure for all of us. None of us wants to run the risk alone. To do so would be foolish.

"What we can do is cooperate. There are ten of us. Each of us can put up one-tenth of the money necessary to send a ship to Africa and then on to the colony in America. If the new trade is profitable, each of us will receive one-tenth of the profits. If the new adventure fails, each of us will only lose a little bit of our wealth.

"All we need to do, gentlemen, is form a stock company. We could call it the New Adventure Company."

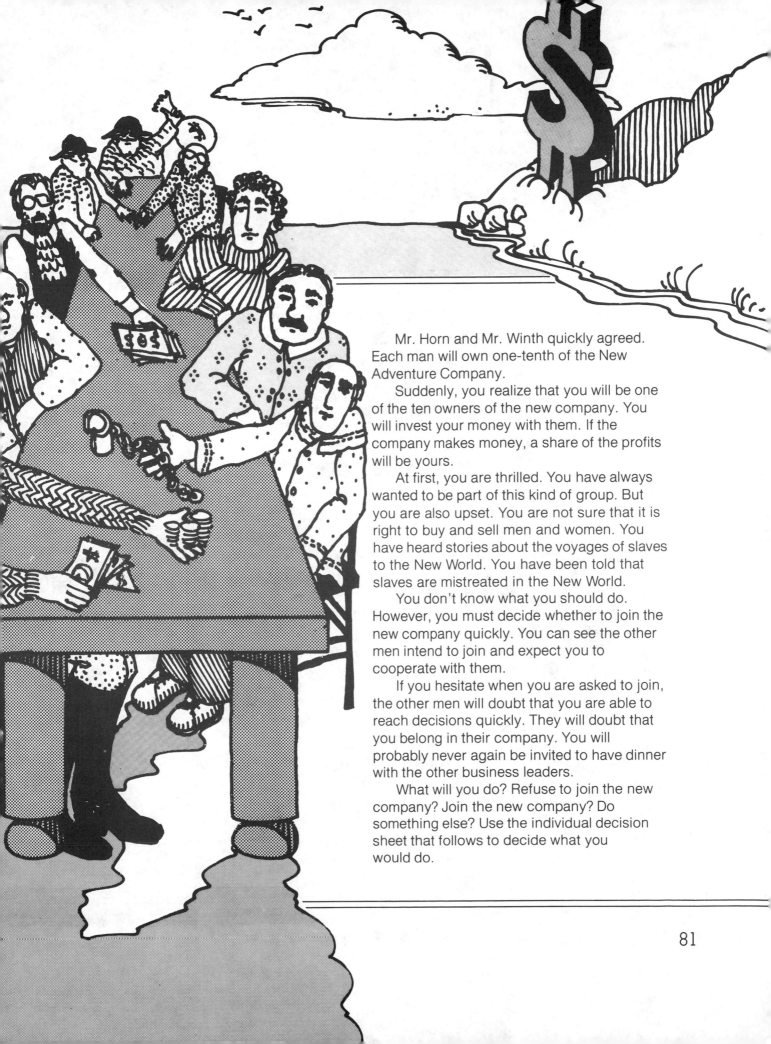

Mr. Horn and Mr. Winth quickly agreed. Each man will own one-tenth of the New Adventure Company.

Suddenly, you realize that you will be one of the ten owners of the new company. You will invest your money with them. If the company makes money, a share of the profits will be yours.

At first, you are thrilled. You have always wanted to be part of this kind of group. But you are also upset. You are not sure that it is right to buy and sell men and women. You have heard stories about the voyages of slaves to the New World. You have been told that slaves are mistreated in the New World.

You don't know what you should do. However, you must decide whether to join the new company quickly. You can see the other men intend to join and expect you to cooperate with them.

If you hesitate when you are asked to join, the other men will doubt that you are able to reach decisions quickly. They will doubt that you belong in their company. You will probably never again be invited to have dinner with the other business leaders.

What will you do? Refuse to join the new company? Join the new company? Do something else? Use the individual decision sheet that follows to decide what you would do.

Individual Decision Sheet

Complete this decision sheet before you discuss it with anyone else. This is to be your *own* work.

List at least four things that you might do in this situation:

A. _____

_____

_____

B. _____

_____

_____

C. _____

_____

_____

D. _____

_____

_____

E. _____

_____

_____

If I were placed in this position, I would do the best thing that I could do. I would _____

_____

_____

My reasons for believing this is the best thing to do in this situation are _____

_____

_____

_____

_____

_____

From J. Doyle Casteel, *Learning to Think and Choose.* © 1978 Goodyear Publishing Company, Inc. Santa Monica, CA 90401

Group
Decision
Sheet

Each member of your group has already made a decision. Now, your job as a group is to make one decision that all members of your group believe is *best* in this situation.

List the choices made by each group member:

It is best to _____
_____

It is best to _____
_____

It is best to _____
_____

It is best to _____
_____

It is best to _____
_____

As a group, we believe it is best to _____
_____
_____
_____

Our reasons for believing our decision is best in this situation are: ___
_____
_____
_____
_____

Members making this decision are: _____
_____
_____
_____
_____
_____

From J. Doyle Casteel, *Learning to Think and Choose,* © 1978 Goodyear Publishing Company, Inc. Santa Monica, CA 90401

Good Better Best

Conceptual focus: Competition

SOCIAL SITUATION

Michael and Sam are both good students. They love their English class, and have always made good grades in that subject.

This year, for the first time, Michael and Sam are members of the same English class. Both have been doing good work in Mr. Johnson's class.

Yesterday, Mr. Johnson returned the first book reports that Michael and Sam had turned in earlier. Both received an A– grade on their book reports—both were disappointed. They were even more disappointed when they found that three other students had received an A grade for their book reports.

On Michael's book report, Mr. Johnson had written a short note. "Your summary of the book is good. But I wanted to know how you felt about the book. You didn't really explain your personal reactions."

Mr. Johnson also wrote a comment on Sam's book report. "I enjoyed reading your reaction to the book. This part was done quite well. Your summary, however, was poorly organized."

After school, Michael went to see Mr. Johnson. He said, "I've always been the best student in my English class. The other students know I'm best. Why are you trying to ruin my reputation? Just remember, I worked hard for it."

Mr. Johnson tried to explain. "I know you are a good student, Michael. In fact, you are one of my better students. But you did fail to write an adequate reaction. I do want to know how you feel about what you read."

When Mr. Johnson went home, he found a note. The note said, "Please call Mrs. Boykin."

Mrs. Boykin is Sam's mother. Mr. Johnson called her after eating dinner.

Mrs. Boykin said, "I am sorry to interrupt your time at home. But Sam is very disappointed. I knew you would want to know. You see, he had always made the best grades in his English class. He's proud of his record. I would hate to see him become discouraged and begin to do poor work."

Once again, Mr. Johnson explained how he had graded Sam's report. "His summary was not organized well."

At the beginning of English class today, Mr. Johnson asked Michael and Sam to work with three other students. The group assignment was to write a short skit illustrating the meaning of the word *fear*.

Almost at once Sam and Michael became involved in arguments. One of the other members of their group tried to get them to stop. She said, "Listen, you two. We've got a job to do. Let's do it."

Sam said, "Michael is the problem. I'm the best English student in here. He knows it. He just doesn't want to admit it."

Michael answered Sam at once, "No, you aren't. I'm the best English student in this class. And before the year is over, I'll prove it."

At this point, still another group member said, "Now, you're both wrong. I happen to know that several people made better grades on their book reports than the two of you did. Who are you trying to kid?"

"My goodness," Mr. Johnson thought. "Both these boys want the other students to think they are best. This competition for grades is out of hand. I must do something, and I must act right away."

Individual
Decision
Sheet

Pretend that you are Mr. Johnson as you complete this decision sheet. Work alone. Do not discuss your work with others until instructed to do so.

At least three things that I might do are:

I might _____
_____
_____

I might _____
_____
_____

I might _____
_____
_____

I might _____
_____
_____

As Mr. Johnson, the best thing I can do in this situation is to _____
_____
_____
_____

The action I recommend is best for the following reasons:
_____
_____
_____
_____
_____

From J. Doyle Casteel, *Learning to Think and Choose,* © 1978 Goodyear Publishing Company, Inc. Santa Monica, CA 90401

Group Decision Sheet

From J. Doyle Casteel, *Learning to Think and Choose*, © 1978 Goodyear Publishing Company, Inc. Santa Monica, CA 90401

Work with other members of your group to complete this decision sheet. Share your individual reactions; decide on one thing that members of your group believe Mr. Johnson should do; and state at least one basis on which you can argue that the decision of your group is best.

List actions recommended by individual members of your group:

A. _____

B. _____

C. _____

D. _____

E. _____

We believe Mr. Johnson should _____

_____

One basis for believing our decision is best is _____

_____

Group members making this decision are: _____

A Ship in Trouble
-A Captain with the Power to Command

Conceptual focus: Power

SOCIAL SITUATION

The time is 1788. You are the captain of an American ship with a crew of thirty-five men, carrying a cargo of wheat and hides. Your destination is a port in Egypt. At the present time, you are sailing between Gibraltar and Egypt; your position is almost due north of the city of Tripoli, located on the coast of North Africa.

Pirates from Tripoli are a constant threat to ships like yours. Some countries pay the governor of Tripoli a tribute on a regular schedule. In return for this tribute, the pirates of Tripoli do not interfere with ships that fly the flag of countries paying tribute.

Your country is not really a country. You are a citizen of the North American state of Rhode Island, a member of the Confederate States of America. The Confederate States of America is a loose union of states which does not pay tribute to the pirates of Tripoli.

Because your ship might be attacked by pirates, you and your crew are ready to fight. Lookouts are watching the horizon for the approach of other ships. Suddenly, the lookout in the crow's nest cries out, "Ship off the port bow. She's flying no flag."

Using your spyglass, you locate the ship—apparently, the ship is in trouble. Most of its sails are gone and you can see other signs of damage. It looks as though the ship has been severely damaged in a Mediterranean storm.

Observing further, you notice that a number of men, a few women, and a couple of children are waving shirts and other objects in order to attract your attention. As far as you can tell, these people are in severe trouble and may die unless you choose to rescue them.

As captain, though, it is your responsibility to protect your crew, cargo, and ship. To meet this responsibility you have been given the power to command your officers and crew.

Quickly, you meet with the other officers who help you command the ship and crew.

One officer says, "It's a trick. Let's sail around those tricky pirates."

Your second officer disagrees. "I see no sign that it is a trick. There are women and children on board that ship. Let's sail to their rescue at once."

A third officer suggests a compromise. "Let's take no chances. Let's send some men over in a longboat. If it's a trick they'll find out. We can't afford to risk all our men. We must find out whether or not it is a trick. It's better to lose a few men and the longboat than it is to lose our whole crew, cargo, and ship."

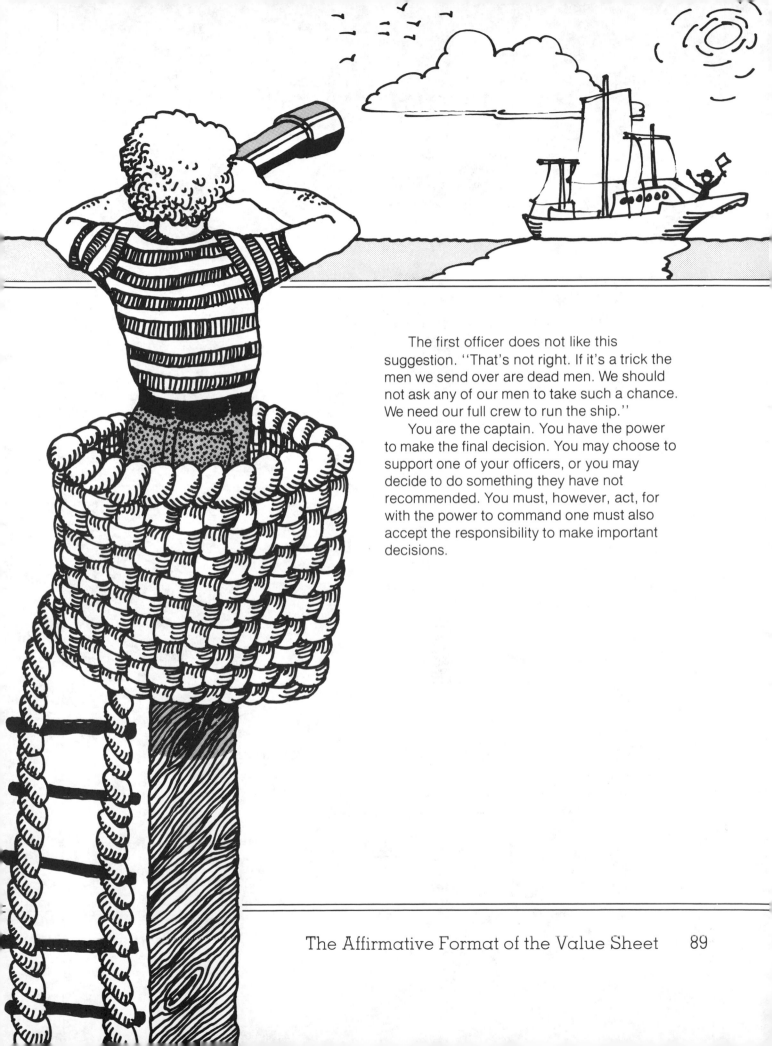

The first officer does not like this suggestion. "That's not right. If it's a trick the men we send over are dead men. We should not ask any of our men to take such a chance. We need our full crew to run the ship."

You are the captain. You have the power to make the final decision. You may choose to support one of your officers, or you may decide to do something they have not recommended. You must, however, act, for with the power to command one must also accept the responsibility to make important decisions.

Individual Decision Sheet

Pretend that you are the captain. List some of the things that you might do in this situation:

A. _____
   _____
   _____

B. _____
   _____
   _____

C. _____
   _____
   _____

D. _____
   _____
   _____

E. _____
   _____
   _____

The best thing I can do as captain is _____
_____
_____
_____

If asked to defend my actions, I would use the following arguments:
_____
_____
_____
_____
_____

From J. Doyle Casteel, *Learning to Think and Choose,* © 1978 Goodyear Publishing Company, Inc. Santa Monica, CA 90401

Group
Decision
Sheet

List the individual decisions made by each group member:

A. _____

B. _____

C. _____

D. _____

E. _____

We believe that the best course of action for the captain to follow is to _____

Grounds that we might use to justify our decision are: _____

Group members participating in this decision are: _____

Snack Time, Meal Time, Decision Time

Conceptual focus: Relative Deprivation

SOCIAL SITUATION

Mrs. Caldwell is a kindly lady of eighty-some years. She lives in a neat little house that is just right for her.

Mrs. Caldwell is a lady of habit. Her daily routine is always the same.

Each morning she arises at six o'clock. She has a piece of toast, two slices of bacon, a bowl of hot cereal, a glass of fruit juice, and one hot cup of coffee for breakfast.

Once the dishes are cleared, Mrs. Caldwell sits where she can watch boys and girls pass by on their way to school. She has a friendly wave and a big grin for each boy and girl.

Having rested, Mrs. Caldwell cleans her house, takes a bath, and then lays down for a brief nap.

For lunch, Mrs. Caldwell has a sandwich, a small bag of potato chips, and a large glass of milk.

After lunch, Mrs. Caldwell makes a daily batch of cookies. Each afternoon she shares her cookies with boys and girls who stop by to see her. For Mrs. Caldwell, this is the high point of her day. She says, ''Talking to youngsters does me a world of good. As long as I can talk and be happy with these youngsters, I will remain young.''

When the cookie snack is over, Mrs. Caldwell again rests for a while.

When she arises, Mrs. Caldwell cooks her evening meal. She always has a small salad or bowl of fruit, a serving of meat, a vegetable, and a glass of milk.

From Monday through Friday, Mrs. Caldwell follows this schedule.

On Saturday, Mrs. Caldwell's daughter picks her up. They go to the daughter's house for breakfast. Then they go to Mrs. Caldwell's doctor to have her blood checked. Mrs. Caldwell must do this each week because she is suffering from high blood pressure.

After leaving the doctor's office, Mrs. Caldwell goes to the drug store for her medicine for the next week, and then spends the rest of Saturday at her daughter's house, returning home just in time for bed.

On Sunday, she spends the entire day with her younger brother.

This week Mrs. Caldwell is faced with a problem. Her blood pressure is up and the doctor has changed her medicine. When she went to the drug store to get her new medicine it cost twice as much as before.

Mrs. Caldwell has a fixed income. She gets a small check each month. This amount is always the same. It does not change from month to month.

In addition, she has a small savings account, which she is saving for serious emergencies.

Mrs. Caldwell does not receive enough money each month to pay for the new

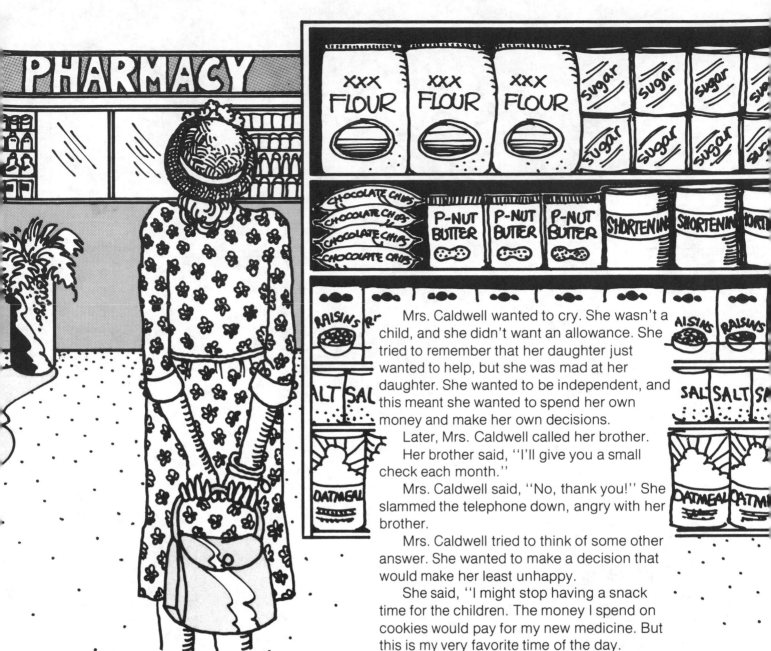

Mrs. Caldwell wanted to cry. She wasn't a child, and she didn't want an allowance. She tried to remember that her daughter just wanted to help, but she was mad at her daughter. She wanted to be independent, and this meant she wanted to spend her own money and make her own decisions.

Later, Mrs. Caldwell called her brother.

Her brother said, "I'll give you a small check each month."

Mrs. Caldwell said, "No, thank you!" She slammed the telephone down, angry with her brother.

Mrs. Caldwell tried to think of some other answer. She wanted to make a decision that would make her least unhappy.

She said, "I might stop having a snack time for the children. The money I spend on cookies would pay for my new medicine. But this is my very favorite time of the day.

"I might stop drinking milk. The price of milk would pay for my new medicine, but I need to drink milk, too."

Mrs. Caldwell thought and thought—she was worried and angry. She believed something ought to be done, something that would be fair.

Finally, Mrs. Caldwell made the best decision she could possibly make. Imagine you are Mrs. Caldwell and complete the decision sheet that follows.

medicine. In order to pay for the medicine, she would have to change her daily habits.

Mrs. Caldwell doesn't know what to do. She tells her daughter, "I don't see how I'll pay for the new medicine. My wants are simple. They have not changed. But now I am no longer able to do the simple things I want to do."

Her daughter replied, "I'll help you, mother. Why don't I give you a small allowance each week?"

Individual
Decision
Sheet

As Mrs. Caldwell, the things I might do in order to pay for the medicine are:

A. _____
   _____
   _____

B. _____
   _____
   _____

C. _____
   _____
   _____

D. _____
   _____
   _____

As Mrs. Caldwell, the best thing I can do is to_____
_____
_____
_____

I believe this is best, because _____
_____
_____
_____
_____

From J. Doyle Casteel, *Learning to Think and Choose*, © 1978 Goodyear Publishing Company, Inc. Santa Monica, CA 90401

Group
Decision
Sheet

From J. Doyle Casteel, *Learning to Think and Choose,* ° 1978 Goodyear Publishing Company, Inc. Santa Monica, CA 90401

Imagine that the members of your group are the children who have cookies each day with Mrs. Caldwell as you complete this decision sheet.

List the individual decisions of each group member here:

A. _____
_____

B. _____
_____

C. _____
_____

D. _____
_____

E. _____
_____

We believe Mrs. Caldwell should _____
_____
_____
_____

Our reasons for believing our decision is best are:
_____
_____
_____
_____

Group members making this decision are: _____
_____
_____
_____
_____

From the Teacher's Perspective

Initiate the use of the affirmative format of the value sheet by reviewing the topic, theme, concept, or idea that students are currently studying in your class. Indicate that students should read the short story that comprises the social situation carefully inasmuch as they will be expected to respond to individual and group decision sheets that are based on this situation.

Distribute copies of the social situation and allow students adequate time to read and study this material. As usual, this should be a quiet time free of talk, movement, or other forms of disruptive behavior.

Ascertain that students comprehend the social situation given and that they can identify elements of the situation that are related to the topic, theme, concept, or idea of the focus of study. (Conventions according to which comprehension and relational discussion starters may be phrased are found in Chapter 1.)

Distribute the individual decision sheets. Remind students that they are to complete this decision sheet working individually. Stress the desirability of listing as many options as possible. Walk around the room in order to determine that students understand the assignment and are following directions.

When students have finished the individual decision sheet, organize them into small groups. Assign students numbers or use some other technique to obtain groups that cut across informal classroom groups and cliques.

Prior to distributing the group decision sheet, define the responsibilities of each group. These are: (1) to share individual reactions; (2) to seek a group position; and (3) to articulate a rationale that justifies the position adopted by the group.

Distribute group decision sheets on which each group may record its work. If you wish, each group may select a recorder. Monitor groups to ascertain that members of the group do participate and that the behavior of group members is task-related.

After the small groups have completed the group decision sheet, close the activity. During closure do at least two things. First, ask one member of each group to share that group's work with other class members. Encourage members of other groups to listen carefully to determine how each group's decision differs from the decision made by members of his group and to determine how they chose to justify their belief that they have made the best decision. Second, review the current focus of study and highlight aspects of the value clarification exercise that are noteworthy in relationship to this focus.

On Your Own

To write your own examples of the affirmative format of the value sheet:

1. Define or delimit the theme, topic, concept, or idea you are currently studying with students who will respond to your value sheet.
2. Find or write a social situation in which a person or group must make a decision. Supply sufficient information for students to assume the role of the person or persons presented in the social situation.
3. Write comprehension discussion starters that you may use in order to help students understand the social situation.
4. Write relational discussion starters that you may use in order to help students frame relationships between the social situation and your focus of study. This is one good reason for beginning your work by defining or delimiting the focus of study toward which you wish to address the value clarfication activity.
5. Write an individual decision sheet. The extent to which detailed directions are required depends on the amount of experience your students have had with affirmative value clarification exercises. If necessary, refer to examples.
6. Write a group decision sheet. Again, the extent to which detailed directions are necessary is dependent on the previous experiences of your students. If necessary, refer to examples.

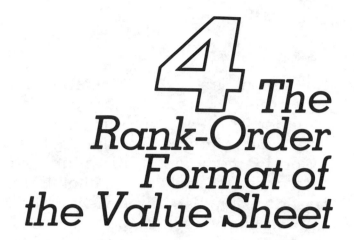

4 The Rank-Order Format of the Value Sheet

Functions

Suppose that there were two individuals who claimed to hold the following beliefs:

○ It is good to be a faithful member of a large and extended family.

○ It is always good to be loyal to one's best friends, no matter the cost of such loyalty.

○ It is good to be truthful and honest in all transactions with other persons.

○ It is good to establish, strengthen, and enforce academic standards.

Both of the persons hypothesized may subscribe with integrity to these four beliefs and yet possess belief systems that are divergent. And this divergence in belief systems may influence the behavior of the two individuals.

The belief systems may differ significantly and lead to divergent behaviors because the two persons assign different values to the four beliefs to which they are committed. A person who places the highest value on being a good member of the family may help a relative cheat on a test or be less than truthful if asked by the police to describe the actions of a first cousin. A second person, who places the highest value on being honest and truthful, may, with some regret, refuse to help a relative who seeks assistance if such assistance violates the norm of being honest.

Individuals and groups that express commitment to the same norms are likely to subscribe to highly divergent belief systems. Although the same elemental beliefs are used to structure their belief systems, two individuals or two groups may quite easily organize these elemental beliefs differently. *The rank-order format stresses the importance of using decision-making skills in groups in order to assign priorities to groups of alternatives.*

Description

The rank-order format of the value sheet contains four components. The first component is a social situation in which an individual or a group needs to cope with a problem. This social situation should provide students with sufficient information so that they can imagine that they are the person or the group described in the social situation. In this respect, the rank-order format does not differ from the forced-choice or the affirmative formats.

The second component is a list of five or more options that are relevant to the social situation. These may be policies that might be adopted in order to cope with a social problem; a list of consequences that might follow from a decision made and described in the social situation; or a list of persons, in conjunction with descriptive data, who are competing for a prize or some other desirable end. The options that comprise the second component are homogeneous, e.g., all are policies, not a mixture of policies and consequences.

The third and fourth components are decision sheets. Each student uses the individual decision sheet to rank order the options given. Small groups of students use the second decision sheet in order to seek consensus with regard to the appropriate ranking of each option. Thus, as is the case with other value sheet formats, individual reactions to a given set of circumstances can become integral elements of the value clarification exercise. Whenever disagreements occur students are instructed to seek a criterion that will enable group members to achieve consensus. Because of the manner in which the rank-order format is structured, members of decision-making groups are likely to apply criterial skill on a number of occasions and on the basis of need. This is to be contrasted with the forced-choice and affirmative format examples which are structured in each instance to require some criterial behavior from students, whereas the rank-order format encourages students to apply criterial skill as such application is vital to the completion of the instructional task.

Classroom Examples
Five examples of the rank-order format of the value sheet are represented here. Study at least four of these in order to prepare yourself to write and use your own examples of this format.

Take Me Out to the Old Ball Game

Conceptual focus: Conflict

SOCIAL SITUATION

Billy and Chuck are members of the same class. Both enjoy sports very much. But they seldom play with one another.

Billy's favorite sport at school is kickball. When the class goes outside to play, Billy quickly organizes those who wish to play kickball into two teams.

Chuck's favorite sport at school is free-for-all dodgeball. When the class goes outside to play, Chuck grabs a ball at once and starts a game of dodgeball.

This worked well until yesterday when one of the players kicked the ball quite hard. Almost immediately the ball was flat. This left only one ball for the class to play with.

When it was time to go outside and play today, Billy tried to grab the one remaining ball for a game of kickball. Chuck tried to grab the only ball for dodgeball players.

Billy grabbed the ball first. Chuck knocked the ball out of Billy's hands. Billy grabbed it back.

Chuck said, "If you don't give me the ball, I'm going to hit you. You'd better let me have it right now."

Billy answered, "We'll see about that. I had the ball first. If you want to fight, I'm ready."

Chuck said, "People playing kickball ruined the other ball. This is the ball for playing dodgeball."

Quickly, other members of the class surrounded the two boys. Those who wanted to play kickball were on Billy's side. Those who wanted to play dodgeball were on Chuck's side. Others were there expecting to see a fight.

Neither Chuck nor Billy could back down now. If Chuck let Billy keep the ball, his friends would say he was afraid. If Billy gave in to Chuck, his friends would say he was afraid.

Soon, Billy and Chuck did what they thought they had to do—they started to fight. Those who supported Billy cheered for him and those who supported Chuck cheered for him.

The noise attracted Miss Ramirez's attention. She arrived on the run to break up the fight. When the fight stopped, she took the whole class back into the classroom. Then she said, "We can't have this sort of thing going on. If we are to learn together and play together, we must try to avoid this sort of behavior in the future. I'm not sure what I should do but I'll tell you what. I'm going to write some things that I might do on the blackboard. Then I may ask you for your help in deciding how we can avoid such disputes in the future."

I. I can ask the Principal to

OPTIONS

Miss Ramirez then wrote the following statements on the blackboard:

1. I can ask the principal to send Billy and Chuck home for fighting. When their parents come to put them back in school, they will know better than to fight again.

2. I can say that there will be no kickball and no dodgeball until we have saved enough money to buy a second ball.

3. I can say that there will be no more kickball until the group that wants to play kickball has saved enough money to buy a new ball.

4. I can ask the dean to spank Billy and Chuck. They should be taught that nice boys do not fight.

5. I can say that no member of the class will be allowed to play outside tomorrow.

6. I can refuse to let Billy and Chuck play outside for one week.

7. I can ask Billy and Chuck to promise that they will never fight each other or any other person at school.

Individual
Decision
Sheet

Complete this decision sheet working alone. Do *not* discuss it with other members of the class until you have finished it. Later, you will be allowed to share your opinions with some other class members in a small group.

Miss Ramirez can only think of seven things that she might do. Your assignment is to rank these seven things. Write a "1" by the best thing Miss Ramirez might do; write a "2" by the next best thing Miss Ramirez might do. Keep doing this until you have placed a "7" by the thing you believe is worst.

_____ Send Billy and Chuck home.
_____ Ban kickball and dodgeball.
_____ Ban kickball but not dodgeball.
_____ Spank Billy and Chuck.
_____ Keep the whole class inside tomorrow.
_____ Keep Billy and Chuck inside for a week.
_____ Ask Billy and Chuck to promise not to fight.

From J. Doyle Casteel, *Learning to Think and Choose*, © 1978 Goodyear Publishing Company, Inc. Santa Monica, CA 90401

Group Decision Sheet

Work with members of your group to complete this decision sheet. Try to reach agreement as to the best solution and place a "1" by this option. Try to reach agreement as to the worst option and place a "7" by this possibility. Then use the numbers "2," "3," "4," "5," and "6" to rank the other options.

_____ Send Billy and Chuck home.
_____ Ban kickball and dodgeball.
_____ Ban kickball.
_____ Spank Billy and Chuck.
_____ Keep the class inside for one day.
_____ Keep Billy and Chuck inside for one week.
_____ Ask Billy and Chuck to promise that they will not fight again.

Participating group members are: _____
_____
_____
_____
_____
_____

From J. Doyle Casteel, *Learning to Think and Choose,* © 1978 Goodyear Publishing Company, Inc. Santa Monica, CA 90401

UP A NEIGHBORHOOD TREE

Conceptual focus: Cooperation

SOCIAL SITUATION

For the last four weeks, Rainwood Forest has been a place of great excitement. None of the boys or girls have asked to go the movies. Television sets have not been used until mothers and fathers turned them on. Children have gone to bed early without urging from their parents. No boy or girl has been heard to say, "I'm bored, there's nothing to do."

Rainwood Forest is a small housing subdivision. All the houses are built on lots that contain large and beautiful trees.

Across the street, there was a second forest. For the last year, men have been building large apartment houses there.

Three weeks ago, one of the boys, Tommy, noticed that a great deal of old lumber was piled up outside one of the apartment buildings. He asked one of the workers, "What are you going to do with this lumber?"

"Burn it," the worker answered.

"May I have it?" Tommy asked.

"And what would you do with it?"

"I would use it to build a tree house. Then my friends and I could have a club with our own club house."

"You may have the lumber," the worker said. "But you must get what you want this afternoon. Tomorrow morning I must burn what is left. Men are coming to sow grass and plant shrubs."

Tommy ran home at once. He went from house to house. He asked his friends to help him get the lumber. He told them that they could help him build a tree house. Like Tommy, his friends were excited about having their very own club in their very own tree house.

Soon, twelve boys and girls were moving the lumber to Tommy's backyard. They got more than enough lumber to build a tree house.

The next day, all the children met in Tommy's backyard. They chose a big oak tree as the place to build the tree house. They made a list of the tools they would need. Most of the boys owned hammers, and some of the boys' fathers had handsaws that they could use. Some of the girls borrowed handsaws and hammers from their parents.

They needed a large ladder. Marie's father, who was a painter, had one. When Marie asked, he said, "You may use my ladder on weekends and in the late afternoon."

Tools and wood were not enough to build the tree house. Nails, roll roofing, hinges for a door, and rope to build a ladder from the tree house to the ground were needed. These things cost money.

No boy or girl had enough money to buy nails, roofing material, or a good rope.

Helen made a list of all the things that were needed:

Nails	$6.50
Rope	$4.50
Roofing	$8.19
Hinges	$2.39
Roofing nails	$1.60
Paint	$4.50
Total	$27.68

Carlos said, "Wait a minute. When my father painted the garage, he didn't use all of the paint he bought. He'll let us use it so we won't have to buy paint."

Brenda said, "My dad has a lot of old doors and things. He'll give us some old hinges for the door."

Helen removed these items from her list. "Then we still need $20.79," she said.

All the boys and girls went home and asked their parents for money. When they returned, they put all their money in an old flower pot.

Helen counted the money—together all the boys and girls had $23.18. "This is more than enough," she announced.

For almost three weeks the boys and girls worked very hard. Last Friday, the new tree house finally was finished. It had a good roof, safe door, and the rope ladder worked fine.

On Saturday morning, Tommy and all the boys met in his backyard, climbed up into the tree house, and pulled the rope ladder up after them so that no one would bother them.

The boys decided that they would form a club. They called themselves the Rainbow Boys. They elected Tommy as their first club president.

They also elected a treasurer, who was told to collect five cents in dues each week from every club member. The boys agreed that new boys who moved to Rainbow Forest could join the club but that they must pay an entrance fee of five dollars.

Later, the girls who had helped to build the tree house arrived. They could not get into the tree house because the boys had pulled the rope ladder up after them.

Marie yelled, "Hey Tommy. Throw the ladder down."

Tommy said, "I'm sorry, Marie. We've just formed a new club, and it's just for boys."

Marie said, "That's not fair. You used my ladder."

Brenda demanded, "Give me back my hinges. Then you can keep your old tree house."

Helen disagreed. "No! They cannot keep it just for themselves. We helped to build the tree house. We've got as much right to use it as they have."

Tommy's mother and father heard the argument. When they found out what had happened, Tommy's father made all the boys leave the tree house. Then he said, "I want each of you to ask your parents to meet with me tonight. We'll decide how to settle this matter as a group. Until then, no one is to use the tree house. This includes Tommy."

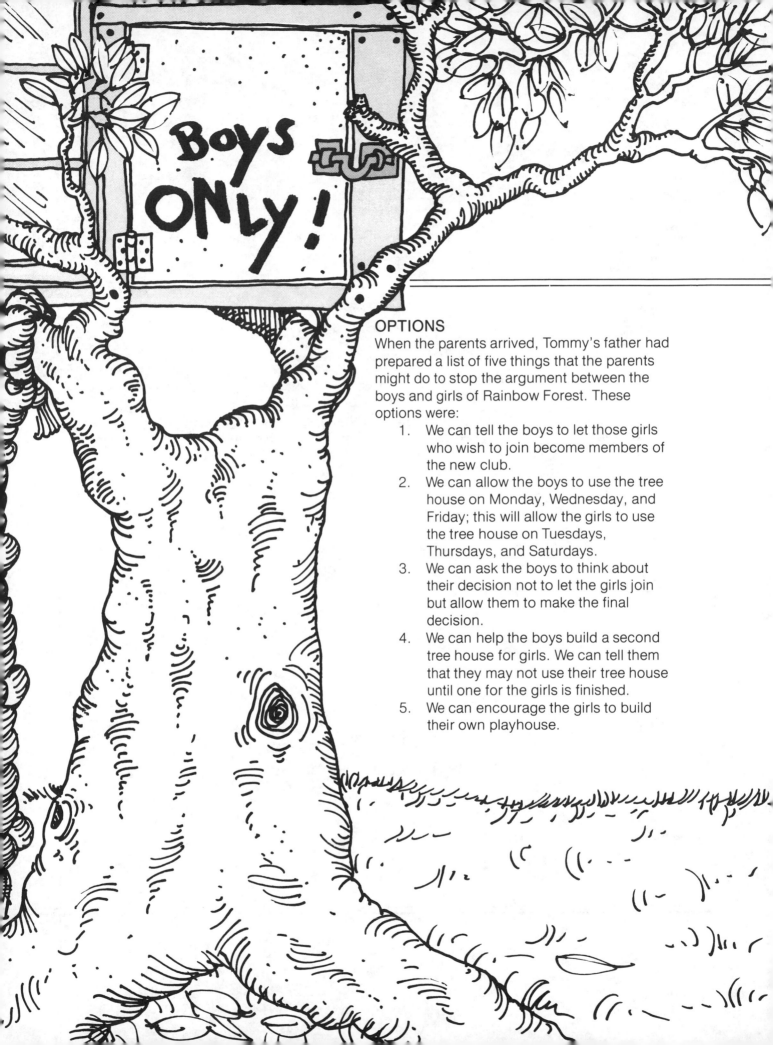

OPTIONS

When the parents arrived, Tommy's father had prepared a list of five things that the parents might do to stop the argument between the boys and girls of Rainbow Forest. These options were:

1. We can tell the boys to let those girls who wish to join become members of the new club.
2. We can allow the boys to use the tree house on Monday, Wednesday, and Friday; this will allow the girls to use the tree house on Tuesdays, Thursdays, and Saturdays.
3. We can ask the boys to think about their decision not to let the girls join but allow them to make the final decision.
4. We can help the boys build a second tree house for girls. We can tell them that they may not use their tree house until one for the girls is finished.
5. We can encourage the girls to build their own playhouse.

Individual Decision Sheet

Work alone in order to complete this decision sheet. As you work, imagine that you are a parent of one of the girls who helped to build the tree house.

Rank order the list of options prepared by Tommy's father. Place a ''1'' by the option that you as a parent of one of the girls believe is best. Place a ''2'' by the next best option. Continue to work in this way until you have placed a ''5'' by the worst option.

_____ Force the boys to accept girls as club members.
_____ Give the boys and girls assigned days on which they may use the tree house.
_____ Leave the final decision up to the boys.
_____ Require the boys to help build a tree house for the girls.
_____ Encourage the girls to build their own playhouse.

From J. Doyle Casteel, *Learning to Think and Choose*. © 1978 Goodyear Publishing Company, Inc. Santa Monica, CA 90401

Group
Decision
Sheet

Work with other members of your group to complete this exercise. Try to agree on the best thing that the parents might do in this situation. Place a "1" by the option that members agree on. Next, try to agree on the worst thing that the parents might do. Write the number "5" by this possibility. Then try to agree on the second best, the third best, and the fourth best options.

_____ Force the boys to accept girls as club members.
_____ Give the boys and girls assigned days on which they may use the tree house.
_____ Leave the final decision up to the boys.
_____ Require the boys to help build a tree house for the girls.
_____ Encourage the girls to build their own playhouse.

Group members making this decision are: _____
_____
_____
_____
_____

Money Isn't Everything

Conceptual focus: Competition

SOCIAL SITUATION

For as long as they can remember, Jane and Sandy have been good friends. Both are seventh graders at West Prong School.

This year, Jane and Sandy were both nominated to be vice-president of the student government. Both were pleased when they were nominated. Both wanted to win but realized that one of them would win and the other would lose.

Jane organized her campaign by getting students in her homeroom to help her. They made posters and badges for her and handed out announcements asking students to vote for Jane.

Sandy's parents helped her campaign by giving her money to hire a professional artist who drew posters for her and having a printer in town print announcements asking students to vote for her. In addition, some members of Sandy's homeroom helped also.

After a short campaign and a school assembly, the students of West Prong School voted. Sandy was chosen to be vice-president—Jane lost by thirteen votes.

After the votes were counted, Ms. Trainer, the principal, told Jane, "You ran a good race. I am proud of you."

Jane answered Ms. Trainer, "I know I lost but it doesn't seem fair. Sandy must have spent more than fifty dollars while I spent almost nothing. It's almost like she bought the election."

Ms. Trainer responded, "There is no rule about the use of money in school elections. Since Sandy won without breaking any of the rules, she is to be the new vice-president of our student government."

"I guess you're right, Ms. Trainer," Jane sighed. "Well, I'll see you around. And thanks."

Later, Ms. Trainer began to think about the election. "It doesn't seem fair. Sandy may have bought the office. We do need some new rules."

OPTIONS

Ms. Trainer then listed several things that she might do in order to avoid the same situation in future elections. These were:

1. I might ask the student government to review election rules at West Prong.
2. I might appoint a committee of teachers to write new election rules.
3. I might write new election rules and ask the student government to approve them.
4. I might leave things as they are. This is the first time we've had this problem. It may not occur again.
5. I might ask a group of parents who are active in politics to write new election rules.

Individual Decision Sheet

Pretend that you are the president of the student government at West Prong School. Ms. Trainer has asked you to rank order the five options she has listed. She wants you to place a "1" by the best policy, a "2" by the next best policy, etc., until you have ranked each of her options. Do this alone. Later you will be able to share your judgments with those of other members of a small group.

_____ Ask student government leaders to review election rules.
_____ Ask a group of teachers to write new election rules.
_____ As principal, write new election rules and ask the student government to approve them.
_____ Leave things as they are.
_____ Ask a group of parents to write new rules.

From J Doyle Casteel, *Learning to Think and Choose*, © 1978 Goodyear Publishing Company, Inc. Santa Monica, CA 90401

Group Decision Sheet

From J. Doyle Casteel, *Learning to Think and Choose*. © 1978 Goodyear Publishing Company, Inc. Santa Monica, CA 90401

Work together to complete this decision sheet. As a group agree on the best policy and place the number "1" to the left of this option. Then agree on the worst policy and place a "5" by this option. Then use the numbers "2," "3," and "4" to rank order the other possibilities.

_____ Ask student government leaders to review the rules.
_____ Ask a group of teachers to write new election rules.
_____ As principal, write new election rules and ask the student government to approve them.
_____ Leave things as they are.
_____ Ask a group of parents to write new rules.

Group members making this decision are: _____
_____
_____
_____
_____

Once Upon a Time

Conceptual focus: Power

SOCIAL SITUATION

Once upon a time, there was a country called Bopland. Bopland was not what we would call a civilized country.

Most of the people of Bopland, called Boppers, could not read or write. Very few Boppers could add numbers together; even fewer Boppers could subtract and divide, and no one knew how to work with fractions. Decimal fractions and percentages had not been invented.

Most of the Boppers lived near the only city in Bopland, called Bop Polis—another way of saying Bop City.

Bop City owned farm lands, pasture lands, and forest lands around the city. Boppers used the grains grown on the farm lands to make bread and the pasture lands to graze cattle, from which they got food and hides. From the forest, they got wood for cooking, building homes, and making tools.

The ruler of Bop City also received tribute from other cities. Each year, cities sent him gifts of wheat, gold, and other valuable things. These were cities that the rulers of Bopland had defeated in wars. If a city refused to pay its tribute, the ruler of Bopland made war against that city.

Because Bop City owned its own farm lands and ruled itself, it was called a city-state. And, because Bop City could force other cities to pay a tribute, it was also called an empire.

Boppers were ruled by a king. Each year all the people paid taxes to their king. When the king went to war, all adult Boppers could be asked to fight. In return, the king of Bopland defended the cities from others and ruled the city.

As ruler, the king of Bopland made all important decisions. He decided what was right and what was wrong. He gave rewards to good Boppers and punished bad Boppers. The people of Bopland said, ''The word of our ruler is our law.'' They were right.

Generally, everything worked fine. Sometimes, however, Boppers who did not get rewards from their ruler complained, and those who were punished felt that they had been treated unfairly.

These people who thought they were punished unfairly said, ''I did not know that what I was doing was wrong. Had I known I would have behaved differently.''

For a long time, no one did anything about this problem. King after king pretended that the problem did not exist. The people of Bopland tried to pretend that the problem was not present. But it was hard for Boppers to forget that they might do wrong and be punished, even when they were trying to do right.

Finally, a ruler of Bopland decided that he would do something about the problem. This ruler was called Boe the Third; also called Boe III by historians.

LAWS OF BOPLAND:

1. IT IS WRONG TO STEAL. IF A MAN TAKES PROPERTY THAT BELONGS TO SOMEONE ELSE, HIS HANDS WILL BE CUT OFF SO HE WILL NOT ... THE PROPERTY ...

OPTIONS

Boe III commanded that a number of Boppers meet with him. He ordered leading priests, men who knew how to write and carve words on stone, and his most trusted advisors to be present.

When all these persons were gathered, Boe III mounted his throne and began to speak. Some of the important things that he said are provided in the quotations that follow.

"Boppers, we have a problem. The problem has been with us for a long time. Boppers break the law and I must decide how they are to be punished. Usually, this works fine. Sometimes, however, those who break the law say that they did not mean to do wrong. They tell me that they did not know that their actions were wrong.

"Many people say they did not know they were doing wrong in order to avoid punishment—these people do not bother me. However, I believe that some of these people are speaking the truth. I do punish people who would not have done wrong had they but known what was wrong.

"When I must punish those who did not know the law, I feel badly. I want to be a fair and good king. I do not want to be remembered as an unjust king.

"I have thought about this problem for a long time. I have discussed it with my priest, with my most trusted advisors, and even with traders who visit our city.

"These people tell me that no ruler has ever solved this problem. Other rulers, like me, are bothered. I, Boe the Third, have decided to solve this problem. I have decided what I will do.

"What we need are some rules that everyone knows. We need to tell everyone what is wrong in Bopland and write our most important laws down so that those who can, may read them. We need to inform all Boppers of the laws and place reminders in important places in Bop City, so that all Boppers may know and obey the law.

"We will begin with six very important laws. These laws are:

"1.   It is wrong to steal. If a man takes property that belongs to someone else, his hands will be cut off, so he will not put his hands on the property of another man again.

"2.   It is wrong to insult our priests, gods, or religion. If a man says a bad thing about a priest, god, or our religion, he will be killed. Those who do not respect our religion will not be allowed to enjoy the good things our gods do for us.

"3.   It is wrong to kill another man. If a Bopper kills another man, the killer and all members of his family will be beheaded. The killer shall not be allowed to take another man's life. His name will not be carried forward by his children.

"4.   It is wrong to say bad things about the king. If a man says bad things about the king, his tongue will be removed from his mouth. If a man listens to bad things about the king, his ears will be removed. Those who are caught saying or listening to bad things about the king will not continue to do so.

"5.   It is wrong for any man to refuse to be a soldier and fight. If a man refuses to fight, his arms will be removed. Those who are unwilling to use their arms to carry weapons do not need arms."

Individual Decision Sheet

Working alone, rank order the six new laws of Boe III. To do this, place a "1" by the *worst* law; a "2" by the *next to the worst* law. Continue until you have placed a "5" to the left of the *best* law. (The law that you select as best may be a bad law. You are only saying that it is better than the other four laws.)

_____ It is wrong to steal.
_____ It is wrong to insult our priests, gods, or religion.
_____ It is wrong to kill another man.
_____ It is wrong to say bad things about the king.
_____ It is wrong for any man to refuse to be a soldier.

From J. Doyle Casteel. *Learning to Think and Choose.* © 1978 Goodyear Publishing Company, Inc. Santa Monica, CA 90401

Group Decision Sheet

As members of a group, select the one law that you believe is worst. Place a "1" by this law. Then, select the law that is better than the other four. Place a "5" by this law. Then try to agree on the correct ranking for the other laws. When you have finished, you will probably be able to share your judgments with other members of the class.

_____ It is wrong to steal.
_____ It is wrong to insult our priests, gods, or religion.
_____ It is wrong to kill another man.
_____ It is wrong to say bad things about the King.
_____ It is wrong for any man to refuse to be a soldier.

Members making this decision are: _____
_____
_____
_____
_____

From J Doyle Casteel, Learning to Think and Choose, © 1978 Goodyear Publishing Company, Inc. Santa Monica, CA 90401

HIGH HOPES, BROKEN PROMISES

Conceptual focus: Relative Deprivation

SOCIAL SITUATION

For purposes of this exercise, assume that you are a social reformer living in the United States about 1845. Imagine further that you know a lot of persons like Mr. and Mrs. O'Shea, whom the following story is about. You may also assume that you have the power to try and correct some of the social problems faced by Mr. and Mrs. O'Shea. First, read the story and then respond to the decision sheets that follow.

In the nineteenth century, Tom O'Shea and his family left their home in Ireland. They said good-bye to their friends and boarded a ship for America. After a difficult voyage on a crowded ship, they reached the United States.

In Ireland, Mr. and Mrs. O'Shea had been quite poor. They had no reason to believe that they could provide a good home, schooling, or a good start in life for their children. Then they began to hear stories about the United States—a land of opportunity.

"In the United States there are plenty of jobs. If a man has two hands and is willing to work he is needed."

"In the United States, wages are good and getting better. A man can live well and still save money."

"In the United States, there are free public schools. Every boy or girl who wants an education can get one."

"In the United States, land is cheap. If a family wants a farm, all they need do is work hard for a very few years and save their money."

"In the United States men are free. Every man may believe, think, and act as he sees fit."

These stories convinced Mr. and Mrs. O'Shea that they should migrate to the United States. They arrived expecting to build a very good life for themselves and their children.

Mr. and Mrs. O'Shea were disappointed with what they found in the United States. They were disappointed by many things.

They were forced to live in a crowded apartment house that only had cold running water and only two bathrooms for six families.

People in the United States were prejudiced toward members of the Catholic Church, and Mr. and Mrs. O'Shea were Catholics.

People in the United States did not like the Irish. Mr. O'Shea was often asked to do dangerous jobs, jobs that were too dangerous for other workers.

Jobs were not always available. Mr. O'Shea was always one of the last workers to be hired and one of the first to be fired. After all, he was Irish and Catholic.

The schools attended by Mr. and Mrs. O'Shea's children were crowded as well as being dangerous firetraps. Children of other religious faiths who attended these public schools made fun of the O'Shea children for

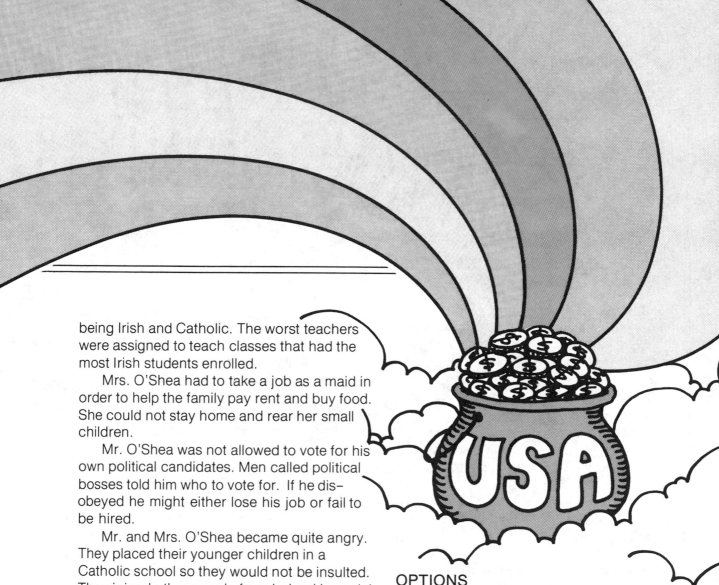

being Irish and Catholic. The worst teachers were assigned to teach classes that had the most Irish students enrolled.

Mrs. O'Shea had to take a job as a maid in order to help the family pay rent and buy food. She could not stay home and rear her small children.

Mr. O'Shea was not allowed to vote for his own political candidates. Men called political bosses told him who to vote for. If he disobeyed he might either lose his job or fail to be hired.

Mr. and Mrs. O'Shea became quite angry. They placed their younger children in a Catholic school so they would not be insulted. They joined other people from Ireland in social groups where they and their family would be treated with respect.

Mr. and Mrs. O'Shea were not happy with their life in the United States. They had wished for a good life they knew they could not have in Ireland. They had moved to America in order to make it possible for them and their children to live a good life. They came expecting that what they had been told about the United States was true.

In the United States, Mr. and Mrs. O'Shea lived far better than they could have lived in Ireland. But they had much less than they had hoped for and expected. They believed that they were *deprived* of things that were rightfully theirs.

OPTIONS

As a social reformer, there are a number of reforms that you might support in order to help people like the O'Sheas.

1. You could fight against the poor housing conditions.
2. You could fight to secure good teachers and good schools for the children of immigrants.
3. You could fight for religious freedom for Catholics.
4. You could fight for improved working conditions for immigrants.
5. You could try to destroy the power of the political bosses.
6. You could fight against the bias North Americans hold toward the Irish.

Individual
Decision
Sheet

Keep the following in mind:
1. You are a social reformer.
2. You do want to help the O'Sheas and others who suffer as they have suffered.

Work alone and rank order the six options from best to worst. When you have finished, you will be expected to share your rankings with other members of a small group.

_____ Fight for improved housing.
_____ Fight for good teachers and schools.
_____ Fight for religious freedom for Catholics.
_____ Fight for improved working conditions.
_____ Fight to destroy the power of political bosses.
_____ Fight to prevent North Americans from holding biased opinions about Irish immigrants.

From J. Doyle Casteel, *Learning to Think and Choose,* © 1978 Goodyear Publishing Company, Inc. Santa Monica, CA 90401

Group
Decision
Sheet

Work together to rank order the six policies that social reformers might work for in the situation described in this exercise.

_____ Fight for improved housing.
_____ Fight for good teachers and schools.
_____ Fight for religious freedom for Catholics.
_____ Fight for improved working conditions.
_____ Fight to destroy the power of political bosses.
_____ Fight to prevent North Americans from holding biased opinions about Irish immigrants.

Group members making this decision are: _____
_____
_____
_____
_____

From J. Doyle Casteel, *Learning to Think and Choose,* © 1978 Goodyear Publishing Company, Inc. Santa Monica, CA 90401

From the Teacher's Perspective

The rank-order format of the value sheet requires more complex student responses than those demanded by the standard, forced-choice, and affirmative formats. Hence, it is critically important to establish and maintain a learning set in which students do not lose sight of the focus of the activity.

Learning sets should contain the following: a review of the idea, concept, topic, theme, or issue that students are currently studying; either an explanation or a related discussion explaining why persons who are committed to the same values or ends may, nevertheless, possess divergent belief systems; and a general overview of the type of decision-making situation in which students are to work. Do not hesitate to take the time necessary to fulfill these functions thoroughly.

Next, distribute the social situation and the list of options that establish the constraints within which students are to perform. At this point, stress the need to study the social situation and the options carefully and maintain a classroom environment free of disruptive behavior in order that students may so study.

After students have studied the social situation and options, use comprehension and relational discussion starters to help them understand the social situation given. By taking this step, you can help students maintain attention to the current focus of study.

When students have demonstrated that they have comprehended the social situation and that they have established its relevance to the current focus of study, distribute copies of the individual decision sheet. When students are working such exercises for the first time, it is necessary to provide careful instructions on how to use numbers in order to rank order objects of valuation. As students gain experience with this type of activity, the need for detailed directions decreases. But when students are asked to respond to such exercises without prior experience, detail is important. As students complete the individual decision sheet, monitor behavior to ascertain that students are following directions and are not discussing their individual rankings.

When the individual decision sheets have been completed, explain that the next task is to seek consensus. Remind students that it is important to listen carefully to one another and to learn to disagree without bickering or insulting one another. Emphasize that where disagreements exist, members of each group should seek some basis other than voting to resolve the dispute. Providing directions such as these between the time that students complete the individual decision sheet and the time that they begin to work in small groups increases the odds that the rank-order format will function as intended.

With clear directions established, divide students into small groups that cut across informal classroom groups and distribute the group decision sheet. As students work in groups, observe their behavior to ascertain that members do participate and listen; that members do make progress toward the completion of the learning task; and that consensus is sought.

To close a rank-order activity, allow one member of each group to share the work of that group with members of other groups. Suggest that students contrast how other groups ranked alternatives with the rankings of their own group. This sharing reinforces the point that values may be organized in different hierarchies. It is also advisable, once again, to review the current focus of study and to highlight some of the ways in which the completed value clarification exercise may be related to the current focus of classroom study.

On Your Own

Use the following steps in order to develop your own examples of the rank-order format of the value sheet:

1. In clear language, state the focus of study toward which you wish to direct the value sheet, e.g., a topic, idea, theme, or concept.
2. Write a narrative in which one or more persons is confronted with the need to assign priorities to a number of options. Provide sufficient information about the individual or group so that role taking is possible.

3. List five or more options that can be ranked from best to worst or from worst to best.
4. Phrase comprehension and relational discussion starters that you may use in order to help students understand the social situation and relate it to the focus of study you identified when you began to develop the value sheet.
5. Develop an individual decision sheet. If students have not had previous experience with this type of value clarification exercise, provide clear directions prior to listing the options. You may wish to shorten the manner in which you originally phrased the options. (See examples of this, above.)
6. Develop a group decision sheet. For groups that are not experienced with this type of activity, provide explicit directions as to the types of student behavior you expect to observe as you monitor the performance of small groups.

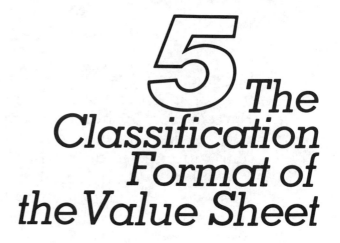

5 The Classification Format of the Value Sheet

Functions

As decision-making groups function, it is not unusual for members of such groups to sort policies they might adopt into three categories. In such instances, decision-making groups tend to classify some policies as most worthy or more imperative. They tend to classify other possibilities as being least worthy or less imperative. And they tend to classify a third group of options as being worthy or imperative but not critically so.

When decision-making groups classify policy options or ends to be pursued, it sometimes becomes important to identify the grounds on which they may establish that those policies or ends identified and grouped as most worthy or more imperative are, in fact, most worthy or more imperative. In such situations, it is also desirable to offer good reasons for rejecting other policies or ends that are judged to be least worthy or less necessary. Whether groups are focusing on rejected options, preferred options, or both, *the task is to generalize items that have been classified according to relative merit and provide criteria that makes the assignment of options to categories appear reasonable and fair to others. The classification format is structured to help students acquire and practice value clarification skills relevant to this type of decision making.*

Description

The classification format of the value sheet contains at least three components and frequently contains four. These are: a social situation; an individual decision sheet which students use to rank a number of options; and one or two group decision sheets that cues and guides groups to classify options into three groups—most preferred, least preferred, and neither most nor least preferred.

The social situation, in common with other formats of the value sheet, establishes a condition within which an individual or a group is to make a decision involving at least nine options. Students may be injected into this situation immediately as they are in the second and fifth value sheets, presented below in the classroom examples. The second value sheet immediately asserts that students in a successful classroom are constantly engaged in acts of cooperation. The fifth value sheet begins with the assumption that all of us, rich or poor, suffer at times from a condition called relative deprivation.

The social situation may also be developed by presenting a set of social conditions and an individual or group that is attempting to cope with the conditions provided. In this type of social situation it is important to identify purposes and constraints and to provide sufficient information about the people who are involved to enable students who respond to the decision sheets to empathize with the persons involved, i.e., to engage in role taking.

The second component of the classification format is an individual decision sheet that contains either nine or twelve options. Students use this decision sheet in order to rank order the options given from the most worthy or imperative to the least worthy or imperative. Except for an increase in the number of options, this component of the classification format does not differ from the rank-order format.

The classification format may contain one or two group decision sheets. If only one group decision sheet is provided, groups are cued to do three things: (1) to select the three or four options that are most preferable in the social situation given; (2) to select the three or four options that are least desirable in the social situation given; and (3) to demonstrate that the preferred options differ from the least preferred options in a desirable manner.

If two group decision sheets are provided, groups use the first decision sheet to identify the three or four most preferred options and to identify grounds on which it may be argued that those options selected are preferable. This may involve the search for a criterion or the identification of desirable consequences that are expected to result from the selection of these options. Groups use the second group decision sheet to identify the least preferred options and to identify grounds that they may use to justify their selection or to analyze possible consequences.

Classroom Examples

Five examples of the classification format of the value sheet follow. In two cases, the second and fifth examples, students are injected into the social situation almost immediately. In the other three, the social situation is quite similar to this component in other value sheet formats. Observe that the rank-order decision sheets always list at least nine options and that either one or two group decision sheets may be employed, depending on how you want students to provide grounds for the manner in which they choose to classify the given options.

As Others See Us

Conceptual focus: Conflict

SOCIAL SITUATION

Lincoln Middle School is located in a large eastern city. When Lincoln first opened about five years ago, all of the students enrolled were North Americans.

Not that there weren't any differences among the students who attended Lincoln. Some of Lincoln's students came from wealthy families, others came from families that had very little money. Most came from families that were in-between—neither wealthy nor poor.

For the last two years, a new group of students has been attending Lincoln. Each year there are more of these students—children of parents who were raised in Latin America.

Recently, teachers have begun to complain about this new group of students.

"These Latin American students all want to sit together. They don't want to make friends with North American students."

"These Latin American students refuse to work on group projects with North American students. It is almost impossible to get them to cooperate. They are always bickering."

"My Latin American students have got chips on their shoulders. They are ready to fight with other students at the drop of a hat."

Mr. Ross, the principal, decided to share his problem with a woman at the local university, an anthropologist. The professor

with whom he talked studies different aspects of Latin American life.

When Mr. Ross explained his problem, the professor said, "Part of your problem is that North American teachers believe a lot of bad things about Latin Americans. If you can remove these stereotypes, it will help you solve your problem. There will be less conflict between North American and Latin American students."

Mr. Ross then asked the professor, "What stereotypes about North Americans are held by Latin Americans?"

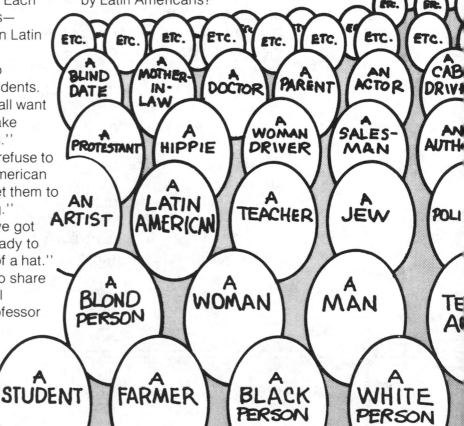

Individual Decision Sheet

The professor identified nine stereotypes of North Americans that Latin Americans tend to believe. Rank order these from the stereotype that would be most harmful to Latin Americans and North Americans who would like to be friends. Place a "1" by the most harmful stereotype, a "2" by the next most harmful one. Continue to rank the stereotypes until you have placed a "9" by the least harmful stereotype.

_____ In North America, nearly all the people are violent. The gangster is a hero in North America.

_____ In North America, nearly all the people want to get rich at the expense of Latin Americans.

_____ In North America, most young people are hippies who use drugs and do other bad things.

_____ In North America, most people are rich. They like to show off their wealth doing foolish things.

_____ In North America, most people are Protestants. They have no respect for the Catholic Church.

_____ In North America, most people do not know how to use good manners. Wives do not keep houses neat. Table manners are poor.

_____ In North America, most people are racists. Blacks, Indians, and other minority groups have no chance to succeed.

_____ In North America, most people support dictators who rule in Latin America. They are for democracy just for themselves.

_____ In North America, most people have no respect for traditional institutions—the home, the church, or the school.

From J. Doyle Casteel, *Learning to Think and Choose.* © 1978 Goodyear Publishing Company, Inc. Santa Monica, CA 90401

Group Decision Sheet 1

Work with other members of your group to complete this decision sheet.

The three worst stereotypes are:

A. _____
   _____

B. _____
   _____

C. _____
   _____

If these three stereotypes were removed, conditions at Lincoln would improve in the following ways:

_____
_____
_____
_____
_____

From J. Doyle Casteel, *Learning to Think and Choose.* © 1978 Goodyear Publishing Company, Inc. Santa Monica, CA 90401

Group Decision Sheet 2

Continue to work as members of a group.

We believe the three *least* harmful stereotypes are:

A. _____
   _____

B. _____
   _____

C. _____
   _____

Now, imagine that the following conditions were true:
1. All the stereotypes except the three you selected as least harmful have been removed at Lincoln.
2. The three you identified as least harmful are still believed by Latin Americans.

If these conditions are true, how might these three stereotypes make it difficult for North American boys and girls to work with Latin American boys and girls?

_____
_____
_____
_____

Nevertheless, these three are least harmful because _____
_____
_____
_____
_____

From J Doyle Casteel, *Learning to Think and Choose,* © 1978 Goodyear Publishing Company, Inc. Santa Monica, CA 90401

Cooperation —a daily occurrence

Conceptual focus: Cooperation

SOCIAL SITUATION

The classroom is a social group. Each of us is expected to be a member of this group. Everyone has reason to want the classroom to be a good place in which to study and learn new things.

If the classroom is going to be a good place to study and learn new things, class members must cooperate with one another and with the teacher.

We cooperate when we share ideas, the things we own, and when two or more of us work together to complete a task.

Nine ways for cooperation in the classroom are listed below. Use the space that is provided after each item to explain why the behavior identified requires cooperation.

1. When we play games, we cooperate. How?_____
_____

2. When different class members do different things to build a bulletin board, we cooperate. How? _____
_____
_____

3. When we do the work the teacher assigns, we cooperate. How? _____
_____
_____

4. When we participate in a class discussion, we cooperate. How? _____
_____

5. When we collect money to pay for a bus and take a field trip, we cooperate. How?__
_____
_____

6. When small groups of students do an experiment in science, we cooperate. How?_____
_____

7. When we help break up fights between classmates, we cooperate. How? _____
_____
_____

8. When each of us brings something for a class party, such as potato chips, we cooperate. How? _____
_____

9. When we plan and do a group project, we cooperate. How?_____
_____
_____

Individual
Decision
Sheet

From J. Doyle Casteel, *Learning to Think and Choose,* © 1978 Goodyear Publishing Company, Inc. Santa Monica, CA 90401

Complete this decision sheet working alone. Nine ways in which members of a class may cooperate are listed below. All nine can be important. Some are probably more important to you than others. Your task is to rank order these from the one that is most important to the one that is least important.

_____ Playing games.
_____ Building bulletin boards.
_____ Completing assigned work.
_____ Speaking and listening during class discussions.
_____ Collecting money for field trips.
_____ Conducting science experiments.
_____ Helping enemies become friends.
_____ Sharing cookies and other good things for a party.
_____ Planning and doing a group project for the class.

Group
Decision
Sheet 1

As a group, we believe that the three most important ways members of our class can and should cooperate are:

A. _____

_____

B. _____

_____

C. _____

_____

If all members of our class cooperated in these ways, the class would be better in the following ways:

_____

_____

_____

_____

_____

From J. Doyle Casteel, *Learning to Think and Choose.* © 1978 Goodyear Publishing Company, Inc. Santa Monica, CA 90401

Group
Decision
Sheet 2

The three *least* important ways in which we might cooperate are:

A. _____

_____

B. _____

_____

C. _____

_____

Suppose members of your class never cooperated in these three ways. How might this make your class a *bad* place in which to study and learn?

_____

_____

_____

_____

These three are least important because _____

_____

_____

_____

_____

The Classification Format of the Value Sheet   137

The Science Teachers' Project

SOCIAL SITUATION

Flagon Middle School contains four grades—fifth, sixth, seventh, and eighth. Flagon Middle School is just five years old.

For the last four years, the science teachers at Flagon Middle School have sponsored a science fair. Boys and girls are encouraged to complete science projects. These projects are all displayed in the school cafeteria.

When the science teachers started the fair, they hoped for two results. First, they hoped that the science fair would make the study of science more exciting for students. Second, they hoped that parents would attend the fair and become better informed about the science program at Flagon Middle School.

The science teachers have been disappointed. Few students have completed science projects they want to display at the fair. Most of the student projects that have been displayed have been poorly done. Very few parents and almost no students have attended the fair.

This fall, the science teachers met to discuss the fair. One teacher said, "The science fair is not working—let's cancel it. It's a lot of work for us, and we're not getting results. It's just not worth keeping."

A second teacher said, "I disagree with what you've said. What we need to do is require student projects. We must require from each student a project that is worth displaying."

A third teacher joined in. "No, we shouldn't cancel the fair. Having the fair is still a good idea. We have got to build up interest on the part of our students.

"Requiring projects is a poor idea. We want students to enter the fair because they are interested.

"What we need is a contest. We should award prizes for each grade. When students realize that they can win prizes, they'll get busy."

The first teacher answered, "I like that. The prizes ought to make the idea of a fair work. If students are competing they'll be more interested."

The second teacher added, "And so will their parents."

The teachers then listed nine prizes that might be used. These were:

A chemistry set

Trophies

A visit to a museum of natural history

Equipment for collecting rocks

A weekend of camping and nature study

A microscope

A nature study kit

An electronic calculator

A citizen's band kit

At this point one of the teachers said, "I don't think we should decide what prizes to offer until we find out how our students would react to these types of prizes."

The other teachers agreed. They, too, thought it would be good to get the opinions of some of the students who attend Flagon Middle School.

Individual
Decision
Sheet

Complete this decision sheet before you discuss it with anyone else. Rank order the prizes from the best to the worst. Place a "1" by the prize that you believe would be most likely to encourage students to enter the science fair. Place a "2" by the next most effective prize. Keep doing this until you have placed a "9" by the least effective prize that might be offered.

_____ A chemistry set
_____ Trophies
_____ A visit to a museum of natural history
_____ Equipment for collecting rocks
_____ A weekend of camping and nature study
_____ A microscope
_____ A nature study kit
_____ An electronic calculator
_____ A citizen's band kit

From J Doyle Casteel, Learning to Think and Choose. © 1978 Goodyear Publishing Company, Inc. Santa Monica, CA 90401

Group Decision Sheet

From J. Doyle Casteel, *Learning to Think and Choose*, © 1978 Goodyear Publishing Company, Inc. Santa Monica, CA 90401

In order to complete this decision sheet, imagine that you are a committee of students that must recommend prizes to the science teachers. Remember, the purpose of the prizes is to get students to become more interested in the science fair.

We believe that the three best prizes are:

A. _____

B. _____

C. _____

We believe that the three worst prizes are:

A. _____

B. _____

C. _____

Some reasons why the best prizes are better than the worst prizes are:

_____

_____

_____

_____

_____

SUSAN'S PLIGHT, DORA'S POWER

Conceptual focus: Power

SOCIAL SITUATION

For purposes of this exercise, you are to imagine that the following things are true:

1. You are a twelve-year-old girl named Susan.
2. You live in Eagle Town, a town of 30,000 people.
3. Until recently, you and Dora were best friends for many years.

Dora lives across the street from your house. For more than two years Dora has delivered the Eagle *Clarion,* the local newspaper. Dora has used the money she made delivering the *Clarion* to buy a new bicycle, new clothes, and once, to visit Disneyland with a group from her church.

When Dora has been out of town, you have been her substitute. You delivered her papers and she always paid you $1.50 each day. For Sunday papers she has always paid you $2.00 because Sunday papers are heavier.

You have always been ready and willing to deliver Dora's papers for her. You have been glad to earn the money and you admire Dora and like to do things to help her. Most importantly, Dora has promised to recommend you as the person to replace her when she quits. She has always promised that she will help you get the paper route.

Three weeks ago, Dora decided that she would deliver the *Clarion* for six more weeks and then quit. She called her boss, the district manager, and recommended that he select you to replace her.

The district manager met with you, your parents, and Dora, and explained the job. He explained how much money you would make each month and how you would pay your bill, and best of all, how you could earn bonus money.

"For each week that you deliver the *Clarion* and no customer complains, you earn an extra dollar of bonus money. If you deliver the paper for an entire month without a complaint, you earn six dollars in bonus money."

Finally, the district manager said, "Susan, the job is yours if Dora tells me you know the route and can do the job when she quits. Between now and the time that Dora quits, you should learn the route, how to collect, and how to keep clear records when customers pay their monthly bill."

At first, you were happy to help Dora roll the papers and place them in plastic bags. You were pleased to carry the papers and

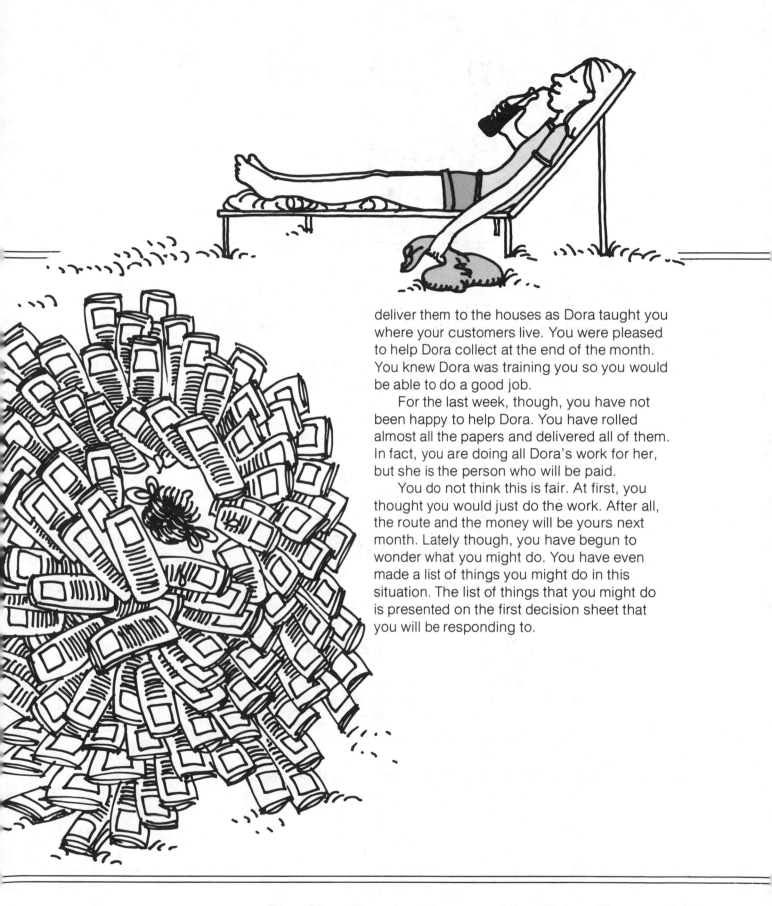

deliver them to the houses as Dora taught you where your customers live. You were pleased to help Dora collect at the end of the month. You knew Dora was training you so you would be able to do a good job.

For the last week, though, you have not been happy to help Dora. You have rolled almost all the papers and delivered all of them. In fact, you are doing all Dora's work for her, but she is the person who will be paid.

You do not think this is fair. At first, you thought you would just do the work. After all, the route and the money will be yours next month. Lately though, you have begun to wonder what you might do. You have even made a list of things you might do in this situation. The list of things that you might do is presented on the first decision sheet that you will be responding to.

Individual Decision Sheet

Working alone, rank order the things that you, as Susan, might do in this social situation. Place a "1" by the most preferable option and continue until you have placed a "9" by the least preferred option.

_____ I might save some of my schoolwork and do it at home. This means that I can tell Dora I would love to help her with the papers but I'm too far behind in my schoolwork.

_____ I might ask my mother to tell Dora that I must help her with housework. This means I will be in the house helping my mother and can't help Dora with the papers.

_____ I might tell Dora I have learned all I need to know and will not help her again unless she agrees to pay me. This means that I will tell Dora she cannot continue to treat me unfairly.

_____ I can continue to do Dora's work for her but tell her she is being unfair. This means that I will let Dora know that she is not fooling me.

_____ I can tell Dora's parents what she is doing. This means that I hope they will make Dora treat me fairly.

_____ I can call the district manager and report Dora. This means that I hope the district manager will force Dora to treat me fairly.

_____ I can tell Dora's best friends how Dora is behaving. This means that I hope they will shame her into treating me fairly.

_____ I can continue doing Dora's work but make a few careless mistakes. This means that customers will complain and Dora will lose bonus money.

_____ I can tell my parents what is happening. This means that I hope they will do something to protect me from Dora.

From J. Doyle Casteel, *Learning to Think and Choose.* © 1978 Goodyear Publishing Company, Inc. Santa Monica, CA 90401

Group
Decision
Sheet

You and other members of your group are to imagine that you are good friends of Susan and Dora. You are to agree on the three best and the three worst things that Susan might do.

The three best things Susan might do are:

A. _____

B. _____

C. _____

The three worst things Susan might do are:

A. _____

B. _____

C. _____

Important and good ways in which the *best* things differ from the *worst* things Susan might do are:

_____

_____

_____

_____

_____

From J. Doyle Casteel, *Learning to Think and Choose.* © 1978 Goodyear Publishing Company, Inc. Santa Monica, CA 90401

Conceptual focus: Relative Deprivation

SOCIAL SITUATION

A person who is deprived wants something he believes is good and something he believes he should be able to have. For some reason, a person who is deprived does not have the ability to obtain the thing he wants.

For purposes of this activity, you are to imagine that you might be *deprived* in nine different situations. Later, you and members of a small group will select the three situations in which you would most prefer to be deprived, if you had to be deprived. You are also to select three situations you would *most* prefer to avoid, if you could only avoid some situations.

In order to complete this exercise, do three things in the following order:

1. Read each situation carefully and then tell why it is a condition of relative deprivation. Use the comprehension guide to record your answers. Tell why you would feel deprived if you were the person in each story.
2. Rank order the stories. Place a "1" in front of the situation you believe would be the worst to find yourself in. Place a "2" in front of the situation you believe would be next worst.

Continue doing this until you have placed a "9" by the best of the nine situations. Use Decision Sheet 1 and do this individually.

3. Work with your group in order to complete the two group decision sheets.

SITUATION A

Abraham has been making a grade of C in his science class. He wants to make good grades. This grading period, Abraham worked harder to make good grades. When he started working harder, a grade of 80 percent was required for a B.

This grading period, Abraham had an average of 84 percent in science.

The teacher said, "Only students who had an average of 85 percent earned a B for this grading period."

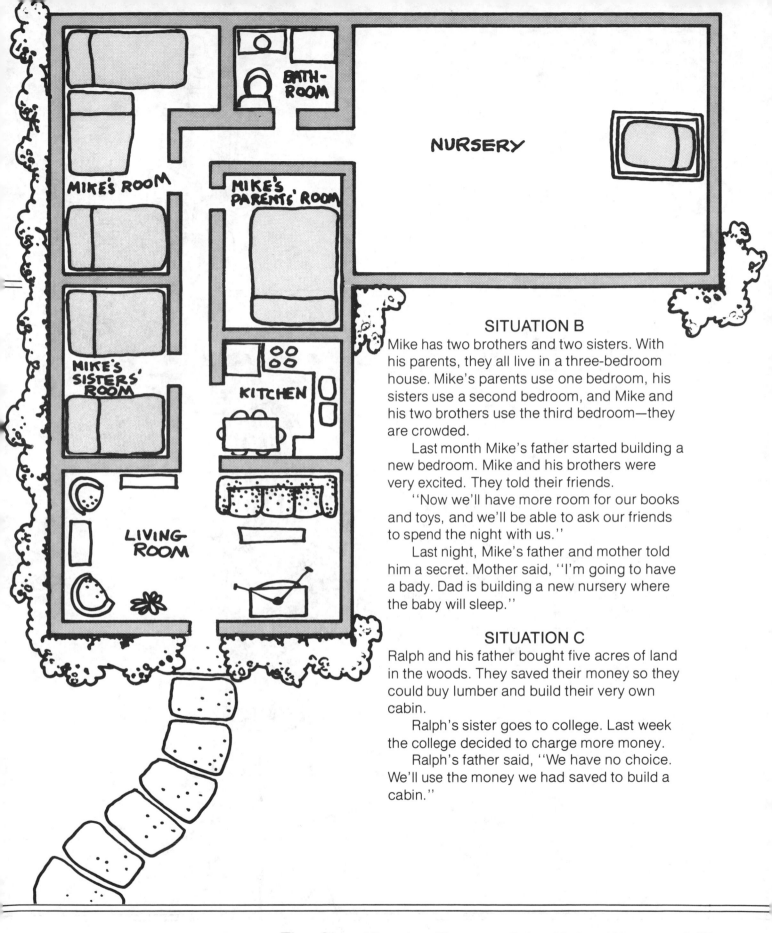

SITUATION B

Mike has two brothers and two sisters. With his parents, they all live in a three-bedroom house. Mike's parents use one bedroom, his sisters use a second bedroom, and Mike and his two brothers use the third bedroom—they are crowded.

Last month Mike's father started building a new bedroom. Mike and his brothers were very excited. They told their friends.

''Now we'll have more room for our books and toys, and we'll be able to ask our friends to spend the night with us.''

Last night, Mike's father and mother told him a secret. Mother said, ''I'm going to have a bady. Dad is building a new nursery where the baby will sleep.''

SITUATION C

Ralph and his father bought five acres of land in the woods. They saved their money so they could buy lumber and build their very own cabin.

Ralph's sister goes to college. Last week the college decided to charge more money.

Ralph's father said, ''We have no choice. We'll use the money we had saved to build a cabin.''

SITUATION D

All the children at East Side Elementary School were quite excited because the school board was building a new library for their school.

The old library was so small and crowded that each class could visit it only once every two weeks. There was no room to go and read magazines or listen to records.

The new library was to be almost twice as big as the old one. There would be room for reading magazines and listening to records, and each class would be able to go to the library very often.

Last night the school board decided more students should attend East Side Elementary School. More than twice as many students as are now in the school will be going to East Side Elementary School next year.

Carol cried when her parents told her what had happened.

SITUATION E

Susan lived near a small stream and wanted to fish in it just like the other boys and girls she watched.

Susan did not know how to fish and since her father did not live with her mother he could not teach her.

Susan's mother said, "I'll tell you what. Go and spend a month of your summer vacation with your aunt who will teach you how to fish."

Susan spent most of the next summer with her aunt and when she returned home, she knew how to fish.

Her mother told her, "Susan, there is a new factory upstream. There are no more fish in the river."

SITUATION F

Steve wanted to get a job delivering papers. He went to the office of a man at the newspaper.

The man at the newspaper said, "You're only ten years old. All our carriers must be eleven years old."

The next year Steve went back to see the man at the newspaper. The man said, "Let's see, you're only eleven. We now insist that all our carriers be at least thirteen years old."

SITUATION G

Last year, all the girls in Sharon's school started wearing bell-bottom jeans.

Sharon told her mother, "I want to have a pair of jeans like the other girls have. They're really neat, Mom."

Sharon's mother said, "We cannot afford to buy new jeans. I'll tell you what. Your older sister will soon outgrow her jeans. When she is too big for them, they'll be yours."

Sharon said, "I suppose I'll have to wait."

This year Sharon wears a pair of bell-bottom jeans to school once a week. All the other girls are wearing shorts and blouses to school.

Sharon tells her mother, "I don't want to wear jeans to school; I want to wear shorts and blouses."

Sharon's mother said, "That's too bad. You wanted jeans, now you have a pair. I just don't know what it takes to make you happy."

SITUATION I

Johnny and his father are great sports fans. Each winter they go to the mountains and ski, and each summer they go to Florida for deep-sea fishing.

This year they decided to learn to water ski. Johnny's father bought a speedboat and water skis, and they both took lessons.

Just when they were ready to start having fun, Johnny's father was asked to go to Central America and work. He told Johnny, "We'll have to forget water skiing for two or three years. How would you like to learn mountain climbing?"

SITUATION H

Wanda is one of the best athletes at Watson Junior High School. All the boys and girls like her to be on their team. She is a good hitter, throws a softball farther than any of the students, and runs faster than anyone else.

But Wanda is angry and disappointed. When there is a school dance, none of the boys ask her to dance. The boys that want her to play on their teams try to avoid her at school dances.

Last year, Wanda noticed that the boys really liked cheerleaders. All the boys wanted to dance with cheerleaders.

Wanda practiced and went out for cheerleader. She was elected, and is now a cheerleader. Still, all the boys want her to be on their softball team. None of the boys invited her to dance at the last school dance. She is still a pal and never an attractive girl to the boys.

Comprehension
Guide

Situation A is an example of relative deprivation because _____
_____
_____
_____
_____

Situation B is an example of relative deprivation because _____
_____
_____
_____
_____

Situation C is an example of relative deprivation because _____
_____
_____
_____
_____

Situation D is an example of relative deprivation because _____
_____
_____
_____

Situation E is an example of relative deprivation because _____
_____
_____
_____
_____

Situation F is an example of relative deprivation because_____

_____

_____

_____

_____

Situation G is an example of relative deprivation because _____

_____

_____

_____

_____

Situation H is an example of relative deprivation because _____

_____

_____

_____

_____

Situation I is an example of relative deprivation because _____

_____

_____

_____

_____

From J. Doyle Casteel, Learning to Think and Choose, © 1978 Goodyear Publishing Company, Inc. Santa Monica, CA 90401

Individual Decision Sheet

From J. Doyle Casteel, *Learning to Think and Choose.* © 1978 Goodyear Publishing Company, Inc. Santa Monica, CA 90401

Rank order the following conditions of relative deprivation. Mark the story showing the *worst* deprivation with a ''1''; mark the story that is next to *worst* with a ''2.'' Keep doing this until you have marked the situation that is most preferable with a ''9.'' Do this *individually.*

_____ Abraham
_____ Mike
_____ Ralph
_____ Carol
_____ Susan
_____ Steve
_____ Sharon
_____ Wanda
_____ Johnny

Group
Decision
Sheet 1

You and other members of your group are to imagine that you must suffer from relative deprivation as three of the boys and girls in the above stories did. Select the three conditions you would choose to experience if this were the case.

If one had to suffer from relative deprivation, the three situations we would accept in order to avoid the other six are:

1. _____
2. _____
3. _____

What bad effects would you fear if you found yourself in these three situations? (List as many bad effects as members of your group can identify.)

1. _____
_____
_____

2. _____
_____
_____

3. _____
_____
_____

4. _____
_____
_____

From J. Doyle Casteel, *Learning to Think and Choose*, © 1978 Goodyear Publishing Company, Inc. Santa Monica, CA 90401

Group Decision Sheet 2

From J. Doyle Casteel, *Learning to Think and Choose*, © 1978 Goodyear Publishing Company, Inc. Santa Monica, CA 90401

Suppose you and other members of your group could avoid only three of the conditions of relative deprivation. If your group could only avoid three conditions of relative deprivation, which three would you avoid?

1. _____
2. _____
3. _____

Assume you could not avoid these conditions. What *bad* things might you do because you were suffering from relative deprivation? (List as many bad things as members of your group can identify.)

1. _____
_____
_____

2. _____
_____
_____

3. _____
_____
_____

4. _____
_____
_____

The Classification Format of the Value Sheet   155

From the Teacher's Perspective

Classification value sheets may be used much like forced-choice, affirmative, and rank-order value sheets are used. Some of these common teacher tasks are:

1. To provide a lesson set that reviews the topic, theme, concept, idea, or issue that is at the focus of study in the class where the value sheet is being assigned.

2. To distribute the social situation and maintain a period of quiet time in which students may comprehend the social situation and search for aspects that are relevant to the focus of study.

3. To use comprehension and relational discussion starters to enhance student understanding of the social situation and to help students frame relationships between the situation given and the focus of study.

4. To secure individual reactions to the rank-order decision sheet so that students may carry personal beliefs into their group work.

5. To use randomization or some other procedure to organize small groups that differ from the informal social groups that are already present in the class.

6. To monitor the performance of group members in order to intervene, if necessary, and in order not to interfere, if the group requires no assistance.

7. To allow each group to report its findings and how these conclusions were reached to the total class. (Here, those students who are listening should contrast how they worked in their groups with how the reporting group reasoned.)

8. To provide lesson closure that highlights significant ways in which the value clarification exercise is related to the current focus of study in the class.

The group decision sheets are, of course, different from those used in other value sheet formats. When students are just beginning to work with group decision sheets for the classification format, you need to explain very carefully that all members of a small group need not agree as to the relative priority of the preferred options. If, for example, student A ranks an option as being the most preferable and student B ranks the same option as being the third best, the two are in agreement that the option is to be classified as one of the best. Again, when students are just beginning to work with this format, it is usually easier for them to respond to two group decision sheets than it is to one. If two group decision sheets are used, students should first concentrate on the best options and then on the worst options. In contrast, when only one group decision sheet is provided, students must deal concurrently with the best and the worst options—a more difficult task.

On Your Own

By following a few directions and referring to examples of the classification format presented in this chapter, you may write your own examples of this type of value clarification exercise. To write your own examples:

1. Clearly state the topic, theme, concept, or issue that your students will be studying when you use the value sheet.
2. Develop a social situation relevant to the focus of study your students will be studying when you use the value sheet.
3. Within the social situation, present a person or a group that is coping with a social problem.
4. Write comprehension and relational discussion starters for the social situation. (In two of the examples you studied, a comprehension guide was included as part of the social situation.)
5. Develop at least nine options that provide those persons present in the social situation with al-

ternatives. (You may use twelve. If you do, students classify four as best and four as least preferable.)

6. Use the nine options to develop an individual rank-order decision sheet.

7. Write a group decision sheet that focuses student attention on the best options.

8. Write a group decision sheet that focuses student attention on the worst or least preferred options.

6 Once Over Very Lightly

Providing students with an opportunity to develop and apply valuing skills that are applicable in decision-making situations are important goals of instruction in the middle grades. This responsibility does not belong to any single area of study; rather, it is a responsibility shared by teachers who teach different bodies of subject matter such as science, social studies, English, foreign language, and reading.

Value sheets written in five formats are relevant to the goals of helping students develop and apply valuing skills as members of decision-making groups. These formats are the standard, forced-choice, affirmative, rank-order, and classification value sheets.

The *standard* format adds a personalization dimension to the comprehension and analytical skills typically used to comprehend and use information found in standard instructional resources.

The *forced-choice* format provides students with practice in choosing the greater good at the price of other good things or in accepting the lesser evil in order to avoid greater evils.

The *affirmative* format stresses that decision-making groups frequently begin to function by developing a large range of alternatives. This range of alternatives then defines the universe from which a decision is to be derived and that may differ somewhat from the original universe of alternatives.

The *rank-order* format highlights how persons who hold the same beliefs may organize these beliefs into divergent belief systems. Persons representing different social groupings or bearing different cultural assumptions may find themselves in conflict because of the divergent manner in which they organize beliefs that are quite similar.

The *classification* format, as its name implies, emphasizes that decision-making groups often classify objects of valuation into three classes: those that are most worthy or imperative; those that are worthy or imperative; and those that are least worthy or imperative.

In order to write and use a standard format of the value sheet, develop three types of discussion starters to elicit student behaviors. These are comprehension, relational, and value/feeling questions and directions. While using other formats of the value sheet, use comprehension and relational discussion starters to ascertain that students are ready to respond to decision sheets. When groups are sharing how they have reacted to group decision sheets, use value/feeling questions to challenge, clarify, or extend what is reported to the total class. Conventions may be used in order to structure and phrase comprehension, relational, and value feeling questions (Chapter 1).

Value clarification behavior in response to forced-choice, affirmative, rank-order, and classification value sheets is cued and guided by two decision sheets. The first decision sheet is completed by students working individually. The second decision sheet is completed by a small group of students. Divergent reactions to the first decision sheet trigger student efforts to persuade and to find a basis according to which consensus may be achieved.

Small decision-making groups should contain a good mix of students. Random assignment of students tends to yield groups that differ from the informal social groups that exist in the classroom.

Classroom teachers with subject matter responsibilities may write and use value sheets that are directly relevant to the content they are teaching. To do this teachers may refer to the examples and conventions presented in Chapters 1–5.

A number of teaching skills are relevant to the use of value sheets: establishing learning set and providing closure; structuring directions and questions that will help students comprehend and relate the social situation on which value clarification exercises are based; providing clear directions as students move from one form of activity to another, especially to individual and group decision sheets; and monitoring individual and group behavior, intervening as necessary to help students work effectively. Although value sheets are structured to require and allow individuals and groups to work independently, you, the teacher, remain an important and influential agent of learning.